T0253167

Praise for *Why People Do What They Do*

'With this book, Saadi Lahlou has done something we haven't seen before. By analysing thousands of naturally occurring behaviour sequences recorded from small body-worn video cameras (along with relevant in-depth interviews), he has developed an original and highly instructive framework for understanding the factors that drive and shape our conduct in a wide variety of situations. Anyone serious about accounting for and predicting human action needs to incorporate Lahlou's insights into their thinking.'

Robert Cialdini, author of *Influence* and *Pre-Suasion*

'"Yes, change is possible" is the convincing conclusion of this densely packed, yet lightly presented, result of a theory-guided approach, which is deeply rooted in practice and experience. Using a sophisticated theory that presents itself in the guise of common sense, Saadi Lahlou provides us with an impressively rich account of how carefully designed interventions can succeed in changing our most ingrained forms of behaviour.'

Helga Nowotny, ETH Zurich and
Former President of the European Research Council

'Many books chronicle our challenging times and the complex issues we face. What is different about this crucially timely book is that it goes beyond calling for the major necessary changes in direction for the world's populations. Based on understanding why people do what they do, Lahlou provides clear, practical guidance about how to encourage people at scale to adopt the necessary new behaviours required to address the multiple existential crises we face.'

James D. Hollan, University of California San Diego

'This novel approach to behavioural change is based on decades of observational research about how people's behaviours are "channelled" in real-world contexts. It elegantly combines the details of behavioural patterns with the many layers of social and environmental influence.'

Susan Michie, University College London

Why People Do What They Do

Why People Do What They Do

And How to Get Them to Change

SAADI LAHLOU

polity

Copyright © Saadi Lahlou 2024

The right of Saadi Lahlou to be identified as Author of this Work has been
asserted in accordance with the UK Copyright, Designs and Patents Act 1988.

First published in 2024 by Polity Press

Polity Press
65 Bridge Street
Cambridge CB2 1UR, UK

Polity Press
111 River Street
Hoboken, NJ 07030, USA

All rights reserved. Except for the quotation of short passages for the purpose
of criticism and review, no part of this publication may be reproduced, stored
in a retrieval system or transmitted, in any form or by any means, electronic,
mechanical, photocopying, recording or otherwise, without the prior permission
of the publisher.

ISBN-13: 978-1-5095-5949-7
ISBN-13: 978-1-5095-5950-3(pb)

A catalogue record for this book is available from the British Library.

Library of Congress Control Number: 2024931505

Typeset in 11 on 14pt Warnock Pro
by Cheshire Typesetting Ltd, Cuddington, Cheshire
Printed and bound by CPI Group (UK) Ltd, Croydon CR0 4YY

The publisher has used its best endeavours to ensure that the URLs for external
websites referred to in this book are correct and active at the time of going to
press. However, the publisher has no responsibility for the websites and can
make no guarantee that a site will remain live or that the content is or will
remain appropriate.

Every effort has been made to trace all copyright holders, but if any have been
overlooked the publisher will be pleased to include any necessary credits in any
subsequent reprint or edition.

For further information on Polity, visit our website:
politybooks.com

Contents

Part 2 How to change behaviour

Introduction

Dear reader, I should start by explaining why I wrote this book.

I assume that you, like me, want to make the world a better place. To do that, we need to change behaviour. Our own behaviour, and the behaviour of others. In fact, we should also change many things about the way our current socio-economic system works. But can we really make people do what we want them to do? Can we channel how people behave, given how diverse they are? It is indeed possible. Let us take an example.

When you travel by air, from the moment you check in at the airport counter to the moment your luggage arrives on the conveyor belt, you have been so tightly channelled that even your seat and the moment you take a drink on the plane are fixed and predictable. Your behaviour has been predictable in space, in time, in your movements, in the interactions you have, in the documents you fill in and the data you give: you have been channelled all the way through. The same kind of channelling happens when you attend a ceremony, go to a medical examination, sit in a class, go to the cinema, stand in line at the supermarket, drive on the motorway, interact with a hairdresser, a shopkeeper, and so on. Although we are free *subjects*, creatures of free will, individuals in command of our own activity, it seems that we act voluntarily to do exactly what is socially expected of us.

Sometimes we are less channelled, as when we are on a train or a bus, where we are free to choose our seat; sometimes we are more channelled, as when working in a fixed position in a factory. Either way, we follow the script more or less happily. Sometimes we seem not to be channelled at all, as when we walk in the woods. But even then we tend to follow the beaten path.

Interestingly, you probably did not experience these channelled journeys as a continuous and tight control of your behaviour. You probably felt that you were acting out of free will, even though you actually made very few conscious choices yourself. On the plane, you may have decided which drink to choose from the limited alternatives offered by the steward (tea? coffee?), and even then, some choices were almost automatic (sugar? milk?). Perhaps passing through airport security or queuing for boarding was perceived as a constraint, but not walking along the corridors of the airport, passing through doors, putting your bag in the rack, etc., even though these are channelling devices.

And, most amazingly, during the journey you behaved in the same way as all other passengers, regardless of gender, age, nationality, culture, income level, religious beliefs, even personal history or purpose of travel. All channelled. So, there are devices in society that channel behaviour in a predictable way, devices that are more powerful than all the classic individual variables. And such devices are well accepted by people. We can use them to deliberately change behaviour.

My colleagues and I have been working for years to understand how this behaviour channelling is done, using the best observation and analysis techniques available. What we have learned, and how to use the same techniques that societies use, we teach it to a few of the world's best students. But now change has become urgent; we need to act on a different scale. Every member of society should mobilize and implement change at their own level, in their local sphere of influence.

This book is an attempt to share widely the know-how to change behaviour, to empower all those who are willing to be effective changemakers. Hopefully, the coalition of the willing will succeed in avoiding, or at least mitigating, the predicted collapse[1] of societies caused by climate change, resource depletion, conflicts and other crises. This know-how will help those who want to create a better world, or simply a better life for themselves and their environment.

There are already various behavioural approaches to changing behaviour (e.g. nudging, boosting). There are also economic measures such as pricing or taxation, and regulation through laws, standards, codes. And last, but not least, there is the design of objects, services and processes. All these are useful, and some are used in various public policies and marketing.

The approach presented here, installation theory, is a big improvement. It shows how to combine the best of these former approaches to increase their impact in a systemic way. It goes a step further by providing a robust method for designing interventions, and explaining how to make change lasting and resilient. In doing so, it empowers the changemaker to reach the best efficiency. How can I make such a bold claim? Because the method draws inspiration from the very mechanisms that societies themselves have set up and perfected throughout history to control behaviour. This is the nut cracked by installation theory: how societies manage to maintain order and evolve at the same time.

Indeed, societies did not wait for the invention of economics or behavioural science to evolve on their own; their speed of adaptation and profound changes throughout history prove that they use powerful, effective mechanisms. A key to this effectiveness is the resilient combination of channelling techniques. It is precisely these powerful systemic mechanisms that we will make explicit here and learn to apply, by finding the best point of intervention in the behavioural trajectory, and the most efficient combination of channelling components.

So, rather than inventing a new approach, we will use the very channelling devices, 'installations', that societies themselves have developed over centuries of trial and error to control and change behaviour. These installations are a combination of channelling components (objects, rules, etc.) that scaffold and funnel people into doing what they do. These components have been deliberately 'installed' for that channelling purpose. In the example of the air travel, the airport corridors, seat number, instructions by the steward, and so on are components of this installation designed for channelling, at the same time supporting and guiding behaviour.

Installations have a momentum of their own: the subjects, after entering the setting, driven by their motive, are taken into a process of feed-forward and feed-back that will channel them into a ready-made behavioural trajectory, as if they had entered an attraction in an amusement park. Installations bring together the tensor of propensities that drive, scaffold and constrain behaviour. As we shall see, some of these propensities are in the subject (e.g. drives, needs), some in the material context (e.g. the objects' potential for action), some in the social environment (e.g. local rules of conduct).

Societies evolve: today's airports, libraries, shops and factories are improved versions of their predecessors, and this improvement did not happen by chance. We will see how this improvement process, which combines reproduction, resilience, and betterment, can be harnessed. Again, it happens through installations, which enable structures to reproduce – and improve – through practice.

Such channelling devices – the 'installations' and their operation, which we study in this book – are ubiquitous in modern societies. Think of how predictable behaviour is, not only on planes, trains, and buses, but on the streets, in offices, in churches, in hospitals, at family dinners – in fact, in almost every social setting. We will see how installations work, how they are constructed, and how their principles and design can be used to deliberately change behaviour.

The channelling principles are a result of centuries of cultural innovation through trial and error by society members to facilitate and control human behaviour. Today, science and technology are discovering that the millions of years of trial-and-error innovation in the natural evolution of biological species have provided powerful solutions to physical, chemical, and biological problems. Engineers take inspiration from biology to design new materials, devices and systems, an approach called *biomimetics*. What we do here is similar but applied to human behaviour and social problems: we take inspiration from a deep understanding of how societies have built systems to channel behaviour, and leverage this knowledge to design new ones, in a *sociomimetic* approach. It spares us the burden of reinventing the wheel, taking stock of the wisdom (and failures) of millions of people who have gone before us. This is needed at a time when we are facing the greatest challenges our civilizations have ever met, as a result of the short-sighted and harmful exploitation of the ecosystem by our invasive human species. Among other things, we need to change our consumption patterns to be more frugal, and this will require significant behavioural changes in almost all our activities.

Rather than a compendium of recipes, this book is a toolbox that empowers the reader to become a 'changemaker', with the generic skills to design interventions and address any specific problem using the three main ways mentioned above. Anyone can become a changemaker, individually or in a group. I wrote this book in a straightforward way, so that every person, at their level, can be empowered to create change and contribute to the transformation that is necessary.

If we all do our part, we can change the world. All that is needed is knowledge, method, purpose and work.

The changemaker needs a toolbox and a method rather than prefabricated solutions, so it is a toolbox and a method that are provided here. The necessary components can be collected in the field, as I show in Part 2. The book is therefore aimed at anyone who wants to understand and change behaviour – 'changemakers' as we have called them – and these can be individuals, groups, communities, private organizations, governments (local, regional, national). What is explained here can be used to design and implement change at the individual micro level, at the local meso level and, to some extent, at the larger macro level.

I hope that the knowledge given here will be used to change how we behave to become more sustainable and, more generally, to serve the common good. Unfortunately, what I provide here may also be used for less noble or even evil purposes. I hope readers will act in a responsible manner, and I provide some guidelines to this effect in Chapter 4.

A final note before you start: the current book has been stripped of the scientific apparatus in order to make the content easily accessible and operational. References are kept to a bare minimum, and examples are deliberately simple. However, the approach is based on a review of the existing scientific literature and on detailed video analysis of the determinants of actual behaviour by real people in real settings. Over the past three decades, my colleagues and I have analysed the determinants of a wide range of activities. Some are as mundane as eating at home or in a restaurant, taking a shower, driving a car or a truck, fixing a flat tyre, cooking, shopping, working in an office or factory; some are complex, such as diagnosing an acute illness in an intensive care unit, conducting a police stop-and-search, or operating a nuclear power plant. Readers interested in a more scholarly approach should consult my 500-page monograph (Lahlou, 2017),[2] with its hundreds of real-life examples and 750 scientific references.

The book has two parts.

Part 1 (Chapters 1 to 9) explains why people do what they do.
Part 2 (Chapters 10 to 14) explains how to change behaviour.

Part 1

Why people do
what they do

1

Applying behavioural change

We do not always act the way we want to, or the way we know we should (e.g. 'bad habits'). We may want to change our own behaviour, and sometimes the behaviour of others. To do this, it is wise first to understand why we act the way we do. This is true for individuals; for example, if we are trying to follow a diet or have decided to exercise more. It also applies to larger groups, from families to large societies – for example, to limit or stop unsustainable behaviour such as CO_2 emissions or pollution. Unfortunately, the solutions that seem obvious (strong will, educational campaigns, public policies) are not very effective – otherwise the problems would already be solved. So, we first need to clarify what the *real* drivers of behaviour are in order to act on them and change behaviour.

The management literature is full of opinionated advice, and there are many (dozens of!) behavioural theories, mostly based on laboratory studies. These are not wrong; they are just not robust enough to create deep and lasting change. Why is this? Most approaches use only a small fraction of the behavioural tools available. They often promote the delusion that behaviour can be changed with a few generic principles, e.g. 'more education', and spare the effort of looking in detail at what causes and sustains the current behaviour, thus limiting the power of intervention. Changing behaviour may not be so complicated, but it does require serious detailed analysis and groundwork. It is naive, and inefficient, to believe that a media campaign alone can change behaviour.

In recent years, successive waves of approaches have emerged in psychology and behavioural science. The 'nudge' approach[1] proposed to frame choices ('choice architecture') in order to steer people in the 'right direction', while leaving them free to choose. This gentle and paternalistic approach can be effective, especially where discrete individual choices are involved and where defaults can be shifted (e.g. the famous shift in defaults in organ donation or pension plans); some reviews show how its effects can be limited in scope, magnitude and time.[2] Nudges are also often low cost (but also relatively low impact). Social norms are an older, but still useful, approach that uses social pressure on individuals.[3] Then, the 'boost' approach seeks to empower people by providing them with skills or information to make better choices.[4] This puts the emphasis on individual choice, which, as we shall see, is only one aspect of the problem. That is why other authors suggest adopting an 's-frame' approach, which considers the societal level, rather than the individualistic 'i-frame' approach.[5]

All these approaches have their merits. Combining multiple layers of components to channel behaviour is even more effective, and that is what societies do. Where complex challenges and social systems are involved (e.g. industrial accidents, sustainable consumption or road traffic fatalities), a systemic and thorough approach is needed to understand and redesign the multiple layers of physical, psychological and social determinants of behaviour to ensure sustainable change. Installation theory provides a systematic framework that facilitates this thorough approach to combine the various channelling components.

The framework described in this book is based on thirty years of empirical research and detailed observation of actual behaviour in hundreds of real-life situations, rather than on laboratory studies or questionnaires. It is based not on what people *think* determines behaviour, but on what *actually* matters. Some of these determinants are straightforward and easy to implement, such as a single choice or time pressure. Others are more difficult to deal with for technical, ethical or political reasons, such as adding social value, coercion, law. We will consider them all, however, and offer advice and caveats where necessary.

An important aspect of this approach, which applies to all types and scales of intervention, is to intervene as much as possible at the place and time of action of the target subjects, the 'point of action', where the behaviour is performed. Intervention there is more efficient. Because that is precisely where the final adjustment and performance of behaviour take place. To use a metaphor, a road sign indicating the direction of a city is more efficient if it is placed at the intersection where you need to turn. Of course, an alternative is to tell drivers in advance where to turn; but if there are no signs at the crossroads, it is likely that some people will not reach their destination easily. What matters most at the moment and place of action is what is *actually* present there. That is what we will learn to design.

While this principle of intervening at the point of action seems obvious, it is not what is done in most classic behavioural interventions. In these, often, people are told what to do, but at a distance from the point of action. That is because it is easier to reach people through the media, rather than at the point of action, where the choice between alternatives is ultimately made, where people buy products, cook, choose a mode of transport, and generally orient their behaviour in one way or another. Think, for example, of recommendations on how to produce less CO_2 or save water and energy: these are often disseminated in a generic way rather than delivered at the point of action. If we want to intervene in an efficient way, we must be prepared to make some effort and not always choose the easiest way, but rather the one that is effective at the point of action.

By point of action, I mean precisely where the target action takes place. Here is an illustration. At the Carnac thalassotherapy centre, customers had free access to two (excellent) detox tea dispensers in a rest area. All customers, most of whom were concerned about environmental issues, took advantage of this free service. Free paper cups were provided next to the tea dispensers, and a poster encouraged customers to use the same paper cup throughout their stay to save the environment (customers are all given bags to carry their towels, treatment schedule and other personal items, as they walk around wearing only a swimsuit and hotel bathrobe, so it is easy to keep the cup in there). A metre away from the dispensers was a rubbish bin. Interestingly, all but a few of the customers drank their tea and then threw the cup away immediately – even though most of them had read the poster minutes before. By midday, the bin was full of cups that had only been used once. Why was this? Because the poster should have been placed at the point of action: on top of the bin, where eyes look just before throwing the cup away. Fortunately, as we shall see, it takes little more than a method and a bit of creativity to intervene at the point of action. For example, other interventions could be providing reusable cups, or removing the bin.

We want to install determinants precisely where and when they can most effectively channel action. Therefore, the changemaker must first understand the activity and its local determinants in order to identify the best points for intervention. Understanding activity and identifying its determinants is the subject of the first part of this book.

2

Behaviour is more or less predictable, and the reason why

Human behaviour (what people do) is predictable. It is extremely predictable in some settings (passengers on an aeroplane), very predictable in others (passengers on a bus), somewhat predictable in others (pedestrians on a street), and less so in more private settings (citizens in their homes).

Why? This difference in predictability follows the functional needs of society. Predictability of individual behaviour, understood here as compliance with expectations, is *indispensable* for conducting activities that require cooperation, such as road traffic or commercial transactions. Cooperation is also essential in most actions of social life. Think of the disruption, even chaos, which can be caused when someone fails to behave as expected in a public place. For example, refusing to pay their restaurant bill, parking their car in the middle of the road, playing ball in a supermarket. Predictability and compliance are essential in complex societies where the need to interact and cooperate is pervasive. This is why keeping one's word and honouring contracts is so important in all cultures.

Moreover, even for activities that are not essentially 'social', societies build specific devices to meet people's needs (e.g. showers, toilets, elevators, vending machines). For these devices to work smoothly, participants should follow some kind of predictable script – and participants expect that if they follow the script, they will be able to perform the activity satisfactorily. This goes right down to the last detail. Consider how disorientated (and perhaps scalded) we can be when taking a shower in an unfamiliar place where the hot/cold water control system is different from what we expect.

More generally, a close look at activities will show that most of them are 'distributed': the global performance is obtained only by combining the contribution of various components that cooperate: the subject, other people, tools, etc. In the case of 'taking a shower', part of the activity is performed by the plumbing system, also by the towel, the bathroom door, the shampoo and all the rest of it. Each component must play its part faithfully and combine gracefully with the expected behaviour of the other components. For example, the shampoo should wash the hair; the person should close their eyes to avoid being hurt, and so on. This need to follow a predictable script also explains why behaviour is more constrained where more exacting cooperation is required for things to go smoothly and without risk, e.g. working in a factory, driving on the motorway, eye surgery, piloting a nuclear plant. There, failure to behave as expected is likely to result in an accident.

For all animals, predictability is important. Animals need to know how others might react to their own behaviour, for example when they want to mate, fight or escape. This is why most animals have developed communication systems. We humans live in complex groups; we have pushed the division of labour, cooperation with others and the redesign of our material environment further than any other species on Earth; our need to cooperate is now very high because we have become extremely dependent on others. Repeated games enable participants to learn that cooperation is worthy,[1] and societies have acknowledged that; therefore they implement rules and other systems to that effect.

So, human societies, in order to thrive as complex, collaborative organizations, have had to build powerful systems to ensure that mutual predictability is guaranteed. That the various components that scaffold behaviour (in the shower, the pipes, the taps, the shampoo, the eyeballs and all the rest of it) fit together and combine as expected. Now that such systems are in place after many trials and errors, we can all, as members of a society, benefit from these previously constructed 'installations'; we can rely on each of us to play our part faithfully and according to the situation, and we can also rely on the objects to play their part, in each and every classic situation of social life: on the street, in class, at the party, etc. Good installations facilitate action by making what is doable at the point of action visible and easy to understand, that is, displaying the 'affordances' of the objects. An affordance is what you can do with the object; it is this object's potential for action.[2] For example, this apple is edible, this window is openable.

This sophisticated and demanding predictability of what we do has an amazing degree of reliability. Take road traffic, for example. In Europe around 2020, there were statistically about six fatal road accidents per *billion* vehicle kilometres (depending on the country).[3] This is less than one fatal accident for every 150 million kilometres driven – the equivalent of driving around the world 3,750 times, which would take a driver centuries. Considering how easy it is to have an accident with a few seconds of inattention or mechanical failure, it seems hard to believe that such a low failure rate is even possible, knowing human nature and especially how reckless some people tend to be behind the wheel. But statistical evidence shows that it is possible. A similarly low rate of 'accidents' can be observed in most human activities: think of crime, industrial accidents, or even more benign accidents such as social scandals. They are very few compared to the number of possible events. Indeed, societies have developed a powerful and resilient system for controlling human behaviour. Of course, there are obviously still areas of behaviour where this behavioural control system has not been applied, or has been applied incorrectly (e.g. diet, energy and water use, pollution).

Finally, it should be noted that what is predictable is what people *do*, not what they *think*. This colleague who works with you may hate you and dream of beating you up! That is fine, as long as he does what is expected of him (cooperate) and behaves properly. As long as we all behave as expected, society can function.

In conclusion, if most human behaviour is so precisely predictable under normal social conditions, it is because society has mastered the techniques of behaviour control. Societies routinely perform, on a large scale and with little failure, exactly the kind of behaviour control that we changemakers are so eager to implement. This fact should reassure the novice changemaker that success is within reach.

Let us now look at some general principles of human activity.

3

From behaviour to activity

First, an important distinction: we must distinguish behaviour from activity.

- *Behaviour* is what the subject does, as observed by an external observer.
- *Activity* is what the subject does, as experienced from his or her own perspective.

For example, an external observer might describe Saadi's behaviour as 'Saadi is walking down the street', whereas Saadi would describe what he is doing (his activity) as 'I am returning home from work.' Clearly, 'behaviour' misses important aspects of the subject's experience.

Because behaviour is a person's activity as perceived by others, it is behaviour, not activity, that primarily matters to others. From the perspective of others, it is my behaviour (what I do) that needs to be predicted and controlled. For example, what matters to someone driving a car on the road is not what other drivers (and pedestrians) think, nor why they are going somewhere, but what they are actually doing, how they are behaving. That is why the powerful social control systems we alluded to in the previous chapter are mostly designed to control behaviour, not activity: to control what people do, not what they think. When we will build channelling systems, we will do the same: channel behaviour only.

This means, by the way, that what you learn in this book will not enable you to change how people think, only what they do. However, because behaviour is an aspect (in a sense a consequence) of activity, and because activity is performed by the subject and from the subject's perspective, it is important to understand the determinants of activity if we want to channel behaviour efficiently. Therefore, we will also try to understand what drives people to act, their motives, their goals, the processes they use to move from one step to the next on their course of action, and so on. In short, we want to understand why people act in order to channel what they do.

The following sections provide some useful concepts for analysing the various aspects of activity, putting in simple words the activity theory initiated by Rubinstein and Leontiev and refined by a century of research.[1]

Motives and goals

People are set in motion by needs, desires and fears; these are a drive to change the current state of things experienced by the subject internally or externally, e.g. to eat, to clean a cluttered and dirty room, to help a relative. So, subjects act driven by 'motives' (what sets them in motion). People have the ability to think. That is, they can represent possible situations and states of things in their minds. When driven by a motive, they usually imagine a state of things that satisfies that motive: e.g. a meal, a clean room, a happy friend. This *conscious representation of a desired state* is a 'goal', which they try to reach, driven by the motive.

Many students, and some professors, initially have difficulty understanding the difference between goal and motive, which has been blurred in Western psychology (I was the same, it took me years to understand). However, this distinction is especially important for our purpose here because goals are easy to change, whereas motives are not. Take the motive 'hunger'. It can be satisfied by different means (e.g. eating a steak, eating noodle soup). You can change the goal (the type of meal), and that is fine, but you cannot suppress the motive unless you satisfy it. You cannot persuade someone to stop being hungry. Feeling hungry, like feeling lonely, sexually aroused, friendly, cold or frustrated, is a biological, animal thing, it is felt; it is not rational, it is part of our bodily nature. And, as we will see in Chapters 7 and 8, motives go far beyond the basic physiological needs: they include social motives, and many socially constructed, 'cultural' motives too, which can feel just as strong.

In this book we will have to acknowledge, time and again, however uneasy that makes us feel, that human beings are animals, social animals, and that, even though human beings do not behave *only* as social animals, they *also* do behave as such. Considering human beings' drives and motives, their propensities as bodily creatures, their feelings and desires will be essential to our endeavour as changemakers because we will leverage these propensities in our work. The motive of hunger will drive the hungry person; therefore, if you manage to connect to this motive the behaviour you want the person to perform, you will likely succeed. For example, you can request people to perform a specific type of behaviour to fulfil their motive (e.g. get in line and pay to get food, provide personal details to get a service).

The motive is a feeling of lack of something, a desire to fill this lack by acting. Hunger is a motive. So is professional ambition, or loneliness. So is, when you look at your dirty room or cluttered desk, this feeling of the lack of order and clarity, for which there is no name, but which we all tend to feel sometimes, at least once our teenage years have passed.

As long as the motive is salient, it keeps driving the activity in a motivation loop. As soon as the motive fades (e.g. when by eating you have satisfied your hunger), the motivation loop is cut and the activity ends. The motive, like any feeling, is vague and difficult to describe. The goal, on the other hand, is clear. It is a conscious representation of what could fulfil the motive. For example, for hunger, a meal; for ambition, a position; for loneliness, a companion.

To achieve the goal, people will imagine a course of action, a 'trajectory' of activity, which will take them from the current state to the final desired state, the goal. This trajectory will take them through steps (subgoals) that gradually bring them closer to the goal. For example, to get a meal, a possible trajectory is: get food, cook, serve and finally eat; to clean a room: make the bed, put scattered things back where they belong, clean the floor. And so on.

These processes are easier to imagine and follow in practice if their path and steps have already been prepared. For example, it will be easy to prepare a meal if we know a shop nearby that sells food, if we have a kitchen with utensils for cooking and a table for serving food. These trajectories are also easier to navigate if the person has the right competence: if one knows where the shop is, how to cook food, and so on. And even better if the same trajectory has already been experienced in the past: the first time you clean a room, you must discover how to do it in the easiest way, for example, which is the best plug for the vacuum cleaner, etc. The next time you clean the room, you can quickly re-use the proven solution, which then becomes a solution 'by default'.

The path usually has many steps. Some behaviour trajectories can be short, for example, going out for lunch. Some trajectories may take years, such as access to a prominent social position that satisfies multiple motives (livelihood, recognition, security, power). In societies, and even more so in large societies, the steps in the trajectory that one must take to achieve the goal can be complicated and sometimes appear as detours. These 'detours' are other activities that have no obvious or immediate connection with the final goal. For example, to reach a high social position, one may have to go through education, hard work and all the rest.

It is important to remember the following structure: the motive (a generic need) 'drives' the subject to undertake the activity. Then, the subject tries to achieve a specific goal that he believes would satisfy the motive. A goal is the final step of the trajectory; it directs behaviour. This is why we speak of 'goal-directed behaviour'. Activity theory summarizes this by saying that 'the activity is driven by the motive and directed to the goal'.

At each step of a trajectory, the subject considers motives and goals, as well as the conditions given by the environment at that point. This process is 'orientation': considering the situation and choosing a course of action. For example, when I arrive at the cafeteria, I will look at the menu and, given the menu, my degree of hunger, and my initial goal (to eat a salad, to have finished lunch at 13:00), considering those 'conditions given' I will choose what to take. In doing so, I may change my initial goal slightly if what I had in mind is not on the menu. My motive is hunger, my goal is to have eaten a salad before 13:00, and the conditions given are the available menu and my food preferences. All these contribute to orient my behaviour into a course of action that will bring the next step in my trajectory of activity.

The difference between goal and motive is key for our purpose. Indeed, if you want to change behaviour, it is relatively easy to change goals, but it is difficult to suppress a motive. Consider thermal comfort: you can change the goal (wear a pullover or switch on the heating), but you cannot suppress the need for body warmth – unless you satisfy it. So, the change-maker should always try to understand the motives underlying the subject's goals. This will open consideration of a set of acceptable alternative goals to which the subject can be redirected and still be satisfied. Keep this in mind: one easy way to change behaviour is to understand the motivation and simply provide either one easier way to achieve the same goal, or another goal that still meets the original motives. In the example of the cafeteria, adding more healthy choices, suppressing the less healthy ones, or offering smaller portions are ways to facilitate behaviour change for those who want to eat, but eat more healthily. These minor changes in objects at the point of action will be more effective than, say, a media campaign urging people to eat healthier but leaving the cafeteria menu unchanged.

This brings us to the interesting notion of 'satisficing', which is different from satisfaction. A satisficing option is one that is 'good enough'. Perhaps another option would be more satisfying (a more comfortable seat, fancy cutlery, the offer of still and sparkling water instead of just tap water). Nevertheless, in the cafeteria, in a context of scarcity, tap water, functional cutlery and decent seating may be enough to satisfice most users, enough to keep them coming back to satisfy their hunger. Satisfaction is different. Satisfaction is the difference between experience and expectations, it has degrees. Satisficing is satisfying minimal expectations. But how much is enough? This is one of these 'how long is a piece of string?' kind of questions we often will meet in installation design. It is an empirical issue: the answer is 'long enough', you have to test in the field.

(By the way, I apologize for always using simplistic examples in this book, like the cafeteria. I trust you, the reader, to think of other examples you are familiar with at work or home: there are installations everywhere and you know them well. But some are easier to use as examples as they do not vary much across cultures. I will re-use some (e.g. the cafeteria) to show various aspects of the same installation, and keep it short.)

The most urgent motives are the most vital, the basic needs (hunger, safety, etc.) They *must* be satisfied for survival. But there are many kinds of motives. For example, one may want to be healthy, to become famous, to avoid an accident. The motives can be positive or negative. It may be confusing that motives can be named either by the feeling that makes us act, positive or negative (e.g. hunger, curiosity, fear) and/or by the kind of satisfaction we want to achieve (security, love, prestige, sleep). But the idea remains the same: to move away from a state of dissatisfaction in a domain in order to achieve a state of better satisfaction in the same domain.

Human beings are animals: we move around in space, unlike plants which must stay in one place. The story of our lives as animals is about moving away from what is bad for us and towards what is good for us. We therefore spontaneously tend to think of action in terms of movement in space. So 'motives' are what make us move away from something and towards satisfaction. Then, in practice, the exact direction (the goal) and the trajectory will depend on the local situation and terrain. It will be opportunistic.

Human beings' basic motives arise from their biological needs: keep physical integrity, breathing, food, reproduction, kin care, . . . Then come the instrumental motives, which concern the means of access to the resources that allow us to satisfy our biological needs. For example, affiliation to a group, having a house, clothes, a source of income. Social aspects are particularly important in humans, as in other primates, and they are not necessarily immediately instrumental: we seek to have friends for the sake of having friends and not just because having friends can be useful.

Still, having friends may indeed be useful in the future, and those who have friends fare better. In the course of evolution, some behaviours had a positive impact in the long term for the species even though their immediate benefits for the individual were not obvious, or even risky. For example, reproduction, exploration, altruism, where costs are certain, but benefits are not. Such behaviours had more chances to be performed if they were coming with immediate reward (e.g. if altruism, or reproduction, also brought immediate reward). The genes of the individuals who enjoyed performing these behaviours *per se* (e.g. who found reproduction or altruism enjoyable) were selected by group selection (groups with such gene pools thrived). Gradually the corresponding drives became part of human species as we know it now; a species who enjoys sex (and hence reproduction), and feels a warm glow in performing altruism. That is why we prefer sweet and fat foods (because they are rich in nutrients); and we have many other drives whose connection to a need is not immediately obvious, but are studied by evolutionary psychology.

Not all drives are innate. There are also cultural drives. These come from education, and shape the ideal self, which everyone tries to become – or to maintain – almost as much as we try to maintain our physical integrity. For example, one will want to have a certain type of social status, of physical appearance ('beauty', that varies across time and cultures), etc. There are also 'values' shared by members of a group. The resources that are useful and important to this group, and the behaviours and instruments that allow these resources to be obtained, are the object of preferences; they are 'valorised', they have *value*. What has value is sought and respected by the members of the group. For example, in a family, or in a hospital, *care* is valued, as well as the people who give it. In a company, *technical competence* and *productivity*, but also *production tools*, are valued. And so on.[2] Gaining more value becomes a motive, whatever the values in our group are.

In practice, subjects are always able to picture and describe their goal. A goal is an explicit situation, object or action that satisfies the motive. For example, if we have sociability as a motive because we feel lonely, then interaction with any friend, or even with a stranger, could be a way of satisfying this motive. And then, because that motive drives us to move, to act, it might become a goal to make contact with such person. This could be making a call to someone we know, or going to a place where we can make contact: a bar, a social network. For the changemaker, knowing the motives and goals of the subject is not so difficult; just a matter of asking the right person, the subject of action or someone who knows them well.

We may feel several motives at the same time (for example, hunger, sociability, and safety). In this case, one motive will usually take precedence over the others. However, people are highly creative in coming up with goals that can satisfy several motives at once. In the example above, 'getting home for dinner' is a goal that could simultaneously satisfy the motives of hunger, sociability and safety. It is therefore not surprising that returning home is such a common goal and that achieving it is such a relief. In fact, most people do it every day.

While the list of goals is endless, the motives seem less numerous. They are probably linked to human nature. Nevertheless, there is no scientific agreement on a complete list of human motives. Motivation theory has been a work in progress for almost a century, and a philosophical problem for as long as philosophy has existed.

In summary, human activity is simple in its principle: driven by a few motives, we try to gain satisfaction by achieving a goal. We determine a trajectory to achieve that goal with opportunism, considering local conditions. An activity trajectory is a sequence of steps we take to achieve a goal, driven by a motive. Each step in this course of action is the task of achieving a subgoal that brings us closer to the goal. The succession of these subgoals will hopefully bring us to the final goal – and thus to the satisfaction of our motive. In practice, these trajectories can be very sophisticated, as we strive to satisfy multiple motives in parallel, mobilizing multiple resources distributed in space and time. This is the story of our lives and, as we have seen, these trajectories are often channelled by society. More precisely for our purpose here, we are interested in how this channelling takes place at the point of action.

Actions and operations

Now that we have understood the generic principles of activity, let us look at how it happens at the point of action, in increasing levels of detail. This will be useful when we need to describe activity, in the process of designing installations.

The subject moves step by step from one subgoal to the next until she has reached the final step (the goal). Getting to the next subgoal is a small problem: a 'task'. A task is resolved by action; e.g. the action 'unlocking the door' resolves the task of achieving the subgoal 'door open'.

Suppose I am, again, driven by the motive of hunger and pursue the goal of going to the cafeteria to have lunch. My successive tasks will be to leave my office, reach the cafeteria, fill my tray with cutlery and food, eat, and return. I will complete each task by taking appropriate actions: deliberate movements and thoughts, e.g. opening the door, picking up a dessert. These actions will depend on what local constraints (door) and resources (dessert) are available.

Each action can then be described in more detail by breaking it down into 'operations'. Operations are automatic, routinized movements and processes that take place beyond the threshold of consciousness. To leave my office, my first action, I perform a series of operations: a few steps to the door, then turning the doorknob. These movements are small automatic steps that my body performs without much conscious reflection. I do them almost without thinking, and certainly without consciously considering which individual muscles I need to use to walk or turn the doorknob.

At the level of operations, the notion of 'free will' is irrelevant, because there is no reflection: it is about automatically chaining small steps that make it possible to go from one subgoal to another. These small operations are physical movements or mental processes that are the elementary building blocks of the activities that we do frequently (e.g. walking, buttoning a shirt, tying shoelaces); these elementary building blocks have been delegated to subsystems in our body that can perform them without conscious supervision, using only peripheral attention. For example, we use automatic mental processes to recognize and decode words and sentences in our language, as when we read a book or a road sign. Unless these operations encounter some resistance and cannot resolve the incoming situation, they proceed and follow one another automatically in a fluid flow. Another example: when we walk down the street, unless we stumble over something or the way is blocked, we usually walk by chaining one footstep to the next. We do this without consciously planning each step in detail. In practice, these automatic mechanisms are triggered as needed by cues and affordances that are set up precisely for this purpose: in the stairwell, the steps follow each other, and our body knows how to go up or down; in the cafeteria, the path follows a functional, pre-determined sequence so that we come across the right cutlery and dishes in succession to fill our tray, and so on. Yes, we do perceive, think, and make decisions for actions, for the larger chunks of activity, but usually not in the detail of the smaller ones.

The more experience we gain, the less conscious reflection is needed to act. An action that has been repeated many times (e.g. turning a doorknob) can become automatic. The subject can then perform it with minimal attention. For example, when learning to drive a car, one must consciously think about the action of changing gear or pressing the brake pedal. After a while, this action is performed automatically, it has become an operation. This operation chains automatically perception into action, in a quick and fluid loop. Interestingly, a similar mechanism applies to the actions of the mind and actions of the limbs. We acquire mental reflexes just as we acquire motor reflexes. Conditioned reflexes (such as pressing the brake pedal when we see an obstacle on the road) are operations, just as are uttering words in our native language or understanding such words.

Activity is not in one mode or another, for example, conscious or unconscious, automatic or decided by free will. It
is a constant blend of all these. Activity is not the product of
separate 'systems' or 'modules' in the brain; it is the product of
a single and intricate nervous system with different nuances
of consciousness and control. Some of these nuances we call
automatisms, some we call consciousness (some say System 1
and System 2).[3] But in practice they always overlap: a human
being is a system of many organs and subsystems operating
simultaneously with varying degrees of mutual awareness
and interdependence. When you discuss important decisions
with your partner, you are not only 'consciously' mobilizing
high-level concepts, at the same time you are also continuously
using 'unconscious' processes to utter words with your vocal
cords, other unconscious processes to interpret into words and
meanings the air vibrations produced by your partner's voice,
and you are colouring these concepts emotionally, based on
your experience and education. In the meantime, and simultaneously, your heart, lungs, stomach – and all the rest of it
– continue to function and have a limited but real connection
with what you are saying and feeling. For example, your heart
rate may vary depending on what the discussion is about.

Each step of behaviour can be broken down into finer sub-
steps until we reach a level of detail that can only be expressed
in physiological mechanisms (neural impulse, muscle contraction, etc.). At the smallest level of detail, such as muscle
contraction or joint flexion during walking, the movement is
usually performed below the radar of consciousness. In cognition, we often speak of 'high level' mental processes, which
are conscious, and 'low level' processes, which are often
unconscious.

Fortunately, we do not need to go into this level of physiological detail for our behaviour change purposes; nevertheless,
it is important to know how things work. Because we understand that, when habits are formed, a significant amount of

activity takes place below the radar of consciousness. Picture activity as an iceberg, where the sea level is the threshold of consciousness. All above that level, we are aware of; but that is supported, continuously, by a vast amount of unconscious processes below.

There is an interesting paradox here, which is also the paradox of complex organizations, of which the human body is one: the higher levels gain global efficiency by delegating detailed control to the lower ones. It is because the body's operations are not subject to the constant attention of consciousness, because the organs can operate autonomously, that resources are freed up for higher level tasks. It is because your body is walking without you having to concentrate on consciously commanding every muscle in your legs that you can talk to your friend while your body is navigating the road. On the other hand, this wonderful ability to delegate micro-decisions to automatic subsystems makes us creatures who mostly operate in default mode (without conscious decision-making), automatically responding to the cues given to us by the local situation. This is why we are so easily 'channelled'.

In summary, the activity trajectory can be broken down into a variable number of steps, depending on the level of detail at which we want to describe it. At a high level, an activity is seen as a single path from an initial state to a final goal, e.g. 'going for lunch'. At a more detailed level, the activity is a sequence of different steps (the sequence of achieving subgoals by performing actions: e.g. from the office to the stairs to the street to the restaurant). And it can be broken down even further by decomposing actions into smaller operations, until we reach a microscopic physiological level of neural impulse and motor contraction that remains below the radar of our consciousness, such as our muscles operating as our legs walk us down the street.

We humans learn quickly and apply what we learn as automatic responses to similar situations, such as opening a door or walking down the stairs. Our behaviour can therefore be easily channelled by the situation ('door in front of us', 'stairs down', and so on) by providing the cues that call for these automatic responses. Of course, in theory we still have a choice (take the elevator or the stairs?). But in practice at the point of action we hardly think about the choice, and our body spontaneously opts for a default behaviour – unless we start thinking about it. The first time we do something ('first exposure'), we learn a how-to-do that can become our default way of doing it. This how-to-do is reinforced by practice and channelled by installations. Still, each time we perform a given behaviour also remains an opportunity to learn and change our habit. We can start to replace the current operations by new ones, and through repeated action we can break this automatism.

Let us now examine how channelling occurs at the point of action.

Orientation and decision

At each step of an activity trajectory, we have the opportunity to take one of several alternatives. Stop or continue, turn right or left, say yes or no, choose a flavour from vanilla, strawberry, chocolate, or perhaps lemon. The generic problem that humans face in life is: 'now-what?'. The circumstances in which this question appears are not theoretical, as in an exam question. In practice, the now-what? occurs in context, with limited time and resources, with usually incomplete information.[4] It is a pressing question that requires a quick response, a response that appears to be 'good enough' to deal with the situation right now: 'Which one?', 'Here?', 'When?', 'More?', 'Which size?', 'Y/N?'; etc. For example, the anaesthetist must choose quickly what to do when the patient cannot breathe (intubation or tracheotomy?). The police officer witnessing a hit-and-run faces a tough now-what?: help the wounded victim or catch the perpetrator? The now-what? can be more mundane: pizza or lasagne?

For example, suppose you are working and a colleague interrupts you. You can choose to answer or not. Once the interruption is over, you can continue with your interrupted task or start a new one, perhaps related to what your colleague has just told you. Such moments of orientation are frequent. We have dozens of such orientation moments per hour, even during the most routine tasks, such as cleaning our house. These moments of orientation are good windows of opportunity for intervention to change the trajectory, because there precisely the behaviour is open to (re-)orientation; e.g. shall I now clean the kitchen or the bathroom? Should I watch this new episode of the series the streaming channel suggests to me?

The orientation moments are the natural joints of activity. At each of these orientation moments, the fundamental problem for living creatures, again, is the now-what? (What am I doing next?) At such moments of orientation, we must take a direction to answer the now-what?. The type of reorientation depends on why we paused for orientation. Perhaps our current task has been completed. Perhaps we encountered an obstacle or interruption. Perhaps a new opportunity has arisen that may change our course of action. For example, as I am cleaning the room, I am interrupted as the vacuum cleaner stops because I have accidentally pulled the cable from the power plug. I orient to understand the problem, see the cable unplugged, fix the problem and continue the task. Then, once the task is completed, I shut down the vacuum cleaner, re-orient and proceed to the next task. In practice, as my student Atrina Oraee showed, these moments of orientation can be identified by behavioural clues: pausing, hesitation, retrying (if the first attempt did not work), sensory exploration of the environment (eye scanning, attentive listening, fumbling, . . .). If we have just achieved a subgoal, we move on to the next step with a new subgoal. If we have not yet achieved the current subgoal, we may continue to work towards the current subgoal, perhaps in a different way; we may also change the subgoal or even the goal.

The actions that emerge from such orientations are not usually thoughtful and deliberate choices in the sense of an explicit weighing of pros and cons ('Should I re-plug the cable or not?' 'Should I answer my colleague or not?', 'Should I continue where I left off or start something else?'). Such 'deliberative decisions' do indeed sometimes occur in activity; e.g. when you need to buy an expensive item, decide what to do this weekend; but they are not so frequent. In everyday life, orientations tend to involve small choices and micro-decisions (such as re-plugging the cable); those tend to be quick, and they are closer to automatic switching than to deliberative decision-making. In most orientation moments, the direction you take is the one you are technically and socially expected to take – not necessarily the one you would have preferred. For example, you will respond to your colleague without deliberating; after being interrupted, you will likely simply visually scan your desk to see 'what there is to do'.

There is, usually, no deliberative choice between several balanced alternatives; rather, there is the main, expected, habitual, default option – or doing something else if the default move does not satisfice. Then the most salient affordance presented in the immediate situation will likely hook you into action. This is because most of these orientations are channelled to make the relevant choice obvious: Which button to press in the elevator? The one with your floor number on it! When should you get off the elevator? When the door opens! And so on. The trajectory is not a series of choices between equally good different branch corridors, but rather a main corridor with small branch corridors.

Perhaps you sometimes find yourself coming home from work in the evening and wondering what it is you have done during the day. Perhaps you realize then that you have not done the important things you had planned, because you have been distracted by a dozen other activities. Our research shows that this is often the case for office workers. Similarly, shoppers often realize on leaving the supermarket that they have bought products they did not intend to buy when they went shopping, so-called 'impulse' purchases. And internet users often end up spending a lot of time browsing useless pages on their smartphone screens, giving away their valuable attention to platform providers. Such behaviours are the result of the chaining of channelled orientations. These orientations were indeed made in 'free will' by subjects, but still they were (deliberately) channelled by design – by your employer, the shop owner, the media platform, who channelled you to do what is in their own interest. Why and how have we been channelled into these minor activities, into these unwanted purchases, into these eyeball traps? What happens at the moment of orientation?

Many theories have tried to model what happens at that moment. Microeconomics, for example, tries to describe it as a calculation of how the 'attributes' of an object provide maximum 'utility'. In psychology, the notion of 'attitudes' tries to describe the strength of a preference for some aspects over others as a permanent disposition of a person. But saying I have a preference for something (e.g. vanilla) simply expresses the higher probability that I do, or choose, that something. It does not explain why.

These classic models describe some typical situations of choice and can even predict some choices, but they do not explain the mechanisms. There is a simple reason for this: the actual mechanisms are extremely difficult to model on paper. That is because they are, *in fine*, biological processes that operate in the flesh; they involve physiology, the physics and geometry of the local situation, and individual variations coming from past experience of the subject, etc. – all things obvious in action but difficult to describe in writing or in mathematical formulas. The mechanisms are not a formal calculation of variables or a value on a scale in our mind. They are the result of the activation of our nervous system, of the way it is wired based on sensory inputs from the current situation and our experience of past situations, education and culture.

Take the case of preference for vanilla. A study explored the preference of adults, in a blind test, for vanilla in tomato ketchup, at doses that are hardly perceivable.[5] It showed that adults who had been bottle-fed as babies had, compared to those who had been breast-fed, a preference for the vanilla-flavoured one compared to the non-vanilla flavoured. That is explained by the fact that infant formula milk manufacturers, who know that mothers tend to taste what they give their babies, had flavoured the infant milk with vanilla in order to make the (unusual) taste of infant formula milk more palatable to mothers. Early exposure of babies to vanilla in rewarding conditions (being fed) had likely built a preference which, as with many food preferences and aversions, is long-lasting. Of course, not all preferences for vanilla come from such early exposures, but this shows how complex and rooted in personal experience our dispositions are.

The process of orientation of behaviour mobilizes billions of neurons, literally; the result of the reverberation of their firings, and possibly their convergence, is the path we ultimately take. A metaphor for this process would be a political election in a democratic process: the outcome is the result of many local discussions and individual contributions, rather than a single top-down logic. To describe realistically how these neural attractors work is beyond the reach of classical mathematical modelling; the way scientists try to approach them now is through other techniques (e.g. simulation and multi-agent modelling), where thousands or even billions of interconnected artificial components try to simulate as a whole what the brain does.

We ourselves are barely aware of our own actual orientation process because it is so complex and mostly unconscious. In motor action, there is no such thing as first a conscious decision to move, then followed by a movement. Encephalography and medical imaging show that there is, rather, a gradual emergence of the motor command in our brains, which we become aware of as more neurons fire in unison. Interestingly, the neuroscience of volition and action shows that the conscious experience of voluntary action occurs only a few hundred milliseconds *after* the action potential actually begins to grow in the brain.[6] So, we only become aware of the motor 'decisions' our brain is making *after* the process has started! This should not surprise us, as we know well that we can act without being aware of having made the decision to act, such as in reflexes; but knowing that this is more often the case than not, and it is not the result of a rational process of decision-making, is a bit shocking.

This means that no logical or mathematical model will ever be able to accurately account for our 'choices', which are a complex, analogous and distributed biological process. A good 'model' would have to be as complex as the brain itself; it would have to be tailored to each individual, and probably consist of billions of elements, as in a real brain. That is not to say that models are useless. They can make predictions based on past behaviour in similar circumstances; they can provide some general and simplified tendencies. And they can help us to consciously influence orientation. Our influence as change-makers will be to drive the orientation in one direction and/or block it in another, by enhancing some inputs in the multiple and diverse flow of factors that intervene to channel the emergence of action.

Fortunately, we do not need to understand everything in detail in order to act. And, from the perspective of the changemaker who wants to channel change, we do not need to understand the details of how things happen in the brain; all we need to do is create an installation that channels behaviour so that, through practice, a new way of doing things emerges.

Let us summarize what we have learned at this stage. A behavioural trajectory is like a journey on a map with many possible roads, where at each intersection the subject chooses a particular path (e.g. elevator or stairs?), following some orientation process. On this journey, the subject is driven by motives, over which we have limited control, and directed towards goals (the endpoint the trajectory is aiming for). Goals are easier to change as long as they satisfy the motives. Figure 1 helps to fix the activity theory in the memory.

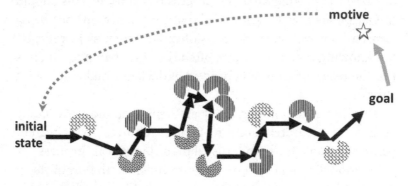

Figure 1 Activity is driven by motives and directed towards goals. The discs represent the channelling components at the various steps of the trajectory. The dotted line shows the motive moving the activity forward.

As we know, we cannot always do what we want. In practice, the subject plans a trajectory (Figure 2). But the actual trajectory might be a tad different, depending on the conditions actually met on the ground (Figure 3).

The moments of orientation are the 'natural joints' of activity. Since the joints are where the subject is open to reorientation, these joints are points where design intervention can channel the trajectory in different directions, if we inject the right determinants. That is not so difficult.

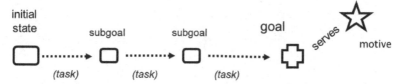

Figure 2 'What the subject wants to do'. Achieving the final desired state (the goal), appears as a series of tasks to solve, to progress, achieving subgoal after subgoal. Once the final goal is achieved, the motive is fulfilled and fades away. Until then, the motive remains salient and moves the subject forward.

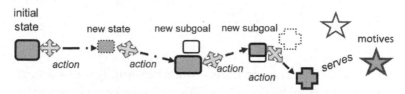

Figure 3 'What the subject actually ends up doing'. In white, the initial subgoals and motive. In grey, what actually occurs, as the conditions given do not always match expectations, and the subject reorients opportunistically, moving subgoals and possibly final goal. The crossed arrows indicate moments of orientation.

One final comment here: there is a ratchet effect in an activity trajectory. For example, once you are seated in the restaurant, it becomes difficult to change your mind and leave, even if you do not like what is on the menu. As an activity develops, irreversible changes happen in various aspects of the situation, and this makes it difficult, possibly impossible, to return or change track. You cannot unlearn what you learned, you cannot reseal the packet of sweets you have opened. Furthermore, as the subject commits to engage in a direction, this very fact will create some commitment for what follows. Some actions will cut, or open, branches of possible futures, strengthening the channelling in a combination of lock-in and opt-out. So, the order in which actions are executed matters more than it seems.

4

The ethics of behaviour and the golden cage of society

Before we consider our means of intervention, it is important to pause and think about ethics. We are in the process of learning how to change behaviour. But should we really change it? Why should we? And if we do, under what conditions?

Ethics comes from the Greek ethos (ἦθος), which means customs and dispositions. Simply put, ethics is about distinguishing between good and bad behaviour, as seen by society: the way we (should) do things around here. Ethics differ from politics. Politics is about how decisions are made in society and how those decisions are implemented in the real world, taking into account the specific characteristics of human beings. More precisely, many political decisions are about 'what to do' and 'how to do it' in society.

The process we are interested in, 'deciding what behaviour we should adopt and how to make it happen', is likely to be a political process that raises ethical issues. By the way, this process might not be obviously 'political'. If a large corporation decides to change its products, this does not immediately appear to be political; but it may become so in practice if the decision changes the behaviour of many. For example, the development of online commerce has not resulted from an overt, collective and public political decision; it has nonetheless changed our consumption behaviour, it has also impacted transport, packaging and pollution. Online commerce generates massive product returns and often destruction of these products because (as in the case of clothing) inspection, cleaning and reconditioning are costly. Online commerce also destroys urban life by putting small shops out of business. These impacts are the result of policy decisions made internally by a few global corporations, involving little informed consultation with end-users. This shows that ethical considerations should be a matter for all actors of change, not just public policy makers.

Now, consider matters of public good, such as the environment, whose conservation requires changing behaviours. Not everyone is ready to change and pollute less. Should we force people to do things they do not want to do? Should we try to influence what people want to do?

Let me present two points that will orient us towards a realistic solution, beyond the classic ethics discussions. The first, the paradox of the golden cage, tells us that living in society is precisely about forcing people to do things and influencing their will. The second, the scarcity of free will, is that the way the problem appears in practice is quite different from the classic approach of free will. As a result, we will see that under certain conditions channelling can be empowering, and that will give us indications regarding how we should operate as ethical changemakers.

The paradox of the golden cage

Look at the big picture. Society already imposes massive conditioning on individuals. Consider how we treat children, forcing them into our way of life and thinking, without leaving them much freedom of choice. We condition them into a

language (which is also a way of seeing things), into many customs (from food tastes to clothing and hairstyles), into obeying
social rules, and even into belief systems such as religions. We
do this in good faith, to adapt them to the current living conditions of society. Nevertheless, we impose intense conditioning
on them, although we prefer the term 'education'. Society (in
fact, we) imposes an astonishing number of conditions and
constraints on each individual; but these are the very conditions for benefiting from being in society.

Living in society is like living in a golden cage: its bars
house us, support us and control us at the same time. We can
choose the shape of the cage and design its bars, but there
must be bars. Please read the previous sentence again; it is the
root of the societal paradox of empowerment through control.
If there was no golden cage to restrict behaviour, anything
goes and life in society would be impossible. For example,
the stronger could exploit and bully the weaker. I know this
exploitation happens already, but less so than if there were
no social control. Without society we would live under harsh
conditions: no golden cage, but no hospitals, no chocolate
bars, no books. We have traded freedom for agency, convenience and comfort.

What should be the shape of the cage? How large? Alas, to
answer that question, there is no longer something like a 'natural state' of freedom we could refer to. Everything in human
societies is, already, to some extent socially constructed,
including the built environment (look around you!), people
and their knowledge and beliefs.[1] We have domesticated not
only many animals but ourselves too; there is no going back
to 'nature', the damage is done. Humans who have not been
raised by other humans cannot even walk on two legs or talk,
as has shown the unfortunate natural experiments of 'feral
children' abandoned in the wild.[2] We humans are an invasive
social species that has altered its environment and niche far
beyond its original ecological conditions.

So, we are left to our own devices to decide what is or is not acceptable as 'how we should behave'. We are free to choose the shape of the societal cage and bars, we are free (as societies) as to how we channel ourselves. In practice, this choice is delegated to (or hijacked by) diverse types of institutions (family, communities, corporations, governments).

This does not mean that 'anything goes'. It simply means that our decisions about what is good or bad are a social *agreement*, within the limits of what is technically feasible. If we were to look only at the biological conditions for the minimum 'liveable' as a standard, that standard would be too low: it would, for example, accept slavery, hardship, poor hygiene. I think we can all agree that higher standards are preferable. However, the fact that there are no clear 'natural' guidelines as to what constitutes 'good' ethical principles is problematic. How should the boundaries be drawn? Should everyone go vegan? Should everyone practise the same religious rituals? What sexual behaviour is acceptable? etc. These are political issues.

Basing 'what to do' on the whim of a single authority (such as a political, religious, or philosophical leader) is not a good option, as history has shown; because there are always divergent worldviews, especially among followers of another ideology. And when diversity is not allowed, this usually results in painful conflict. That is why we need inclusive deliberation and decision procedures that involve and empower all stakeholders.

The scarcity of free will

But how much choice should we leave to stakeholders? Let us now consider the second aspect, the scarcity of free will. Ethical discussions about choice usually revolve around free will, consent, preferences, responsibility, proportionality. But, in fact, the problem may not be well framed because, as we have seen in the previous chapters, most of the time people do not act consciously and deliberately at the point of action. They act in channelled ways.

In practice, for channelled behaviour, free will and choice are concepts that may apply at the level of goal choice but not at all levels of activity. It appears that people have little choice about motives: these arise from physiological needs or social pressure over which one has limited control unless one is a saint or a guru. We can resist motives, but we can hardly suppress them. For example, one can learn to self-control fear, hunger, or sexual urges, but total suppression is difficult. The same limitation to control (in fact: no conscious control) applies to the very fine-grained level of operations (such as interpreting words when we hear them or contracting our muscles when we walk).

On the big map of all the possible behaviours, in practice we only exercise our free will at the main intersections of channelled paths. At the point of action, we are channelled and rarely fully exercise our capacity for free will and choice. Once you have chosen the restaurant where you will go, you are caught into a behavioural stream like the person canoeing in a rapid:[3] your behaviour becomes predictable (even on how you get there) and your further choices are limited by what is available on the menu. And if you prefer to stay at home for dinner, once you have chosen what to eat, the same applies: you will follow the recipe and then the dinner script.

Since a great deal of what we do, at the moment we do it, is not under our personal control and may even happen below the radar of our consciousness, since most of our lives are lived in a channelled mode, the question of ethics appears in a different light. If we want to have free will and reflection, we should make the decisions away from the moment of action, and then at the point of action make sure we act accordingly. For example, the family decides that the children should learn music, and then hires a music teacher who comes to teach them twice a week. When the teacher comes, the child learns – but otherwise that learning would likely not happen. Or if, following employees' request, an organization changes its cafeteria's menu to discourage junk food and puts water jugs on every table, it is channelling behaviour; but, in doing so, it is also empowering those employees who want to act on their 'healthy' eating principles.

Therefore, consciously channelling ourselves can be a way of re-establishing, by default, our conscious and deliberate choice, supporting the act of free will we made at the moment of choosing goals. In other words, we can *self-channel*: we can make ourselves do what we want to do in the future and achieve our goals by preparing an installation that channels us to that effect. For example, if we decide to quit smoking, our problem becomes that of channelling ourselves into actually doing what we have decided, ensuring that the installation supports our decision. Because our will alone is hardly sufficient.

In fact, many installations are deliberately made by people for their own personal use. For example, I consciously self-channel by creating habits that align with my values, such as setting my alarm clock earlier to channel myself to exercise in the morning, or buying a bicycle to commute to work – not to mention filling out my calendar. In those self-channelling decisions, we fully exercise our free will: we weigh our choices, we explore options, we consult expert sources and other stakeholders. And then we consciously empower ourselves to act as we wish.

So, channelling can be a realistic way of empowering people to act in accordance with their own free will and conscious deliberation, by making it easier for them to do what they want to do at the point of action, protecting them from distraction, omission, temptation, influence, etc., at the point of delivery of the behaviour. At the societal level, this is the case: most installations implement (for the individuals) the behaviours that have been socially decided by law or custom, from round-abouts that channel traffic to schools that channel education.

But how far should we go? If the cafeteria also stops offering sweetened drinks (which nutritionists say are not good for health if consumed in excess), it has channelled users in a powerful way not to drink such drinks. Is this going too far? Advocates of the nudge approach say we should always leave people free to choose. I would rather suggest that stakeholders should debate what they want and decide whether the channelling is in the right direction and proportionate to the expected benefits. After all, ethics is always about proportionality, about balancing competing interests.

How to be an ethical changemaker

What does all this mean for the ethics of behaviour change? It means that, beyond respecting basic biological needs, there are no absolute moral standards, and that whatever we do will be a marginal addition to a social system that already imposes massive conditioning on a daily basis. In practice, societies routinely use methods that are sometimes far from gentle: they include propaganda, psychological pressure, rules, coercion, violence, punishment, and simply making some behaviour technically impossible. This is not to say that these methods are recommended; but it does suggest that if changemakers really want to get results, they need not be too picky and shy about the means they use.

On the other hand, we should be extremely clear and reflective about the ends, why we (as a society, but also as changemakers) are doing this, how it is justified, and make sure that the means are proportionate to the end. I will come back to the how in the second part of the book. This divides the ethical question into two aspects, direction and proportionality – ends and means. First, what do we collectively want to do?

Then, how far are we prepared to go in terms of constraints and incentives?

Both questions are a 'how long is a piece of string?' type of question; which means that there is no absolute answer nor a definitive procedure to decide; rather, it will depend on the local situation and conditions, and what your motives are. You will have to play it by ear and be aware that both ends and means will be local compromises in relation to a particular perspective or purpose, a compromise depending on place and time, and subject to power struggles. One must remain modest: reality is complex, decisions affecting a specific case are made in different arenas and involve a set of actors, rules and relationships that are neither completely independent nor completely related. The nut of perfect governance has not yet been cracked, although some progress has been made.[4] So, you have to do your best to collaborate with stakeholders to find a solution that improves the target activity, a solution that is 'good enough' in most other respects, and avoids or compensates for collateral damage. The mistake would be to think it is easy and to neglect the phases of considering potential difficulties and consulting stakeholders before making a decision.

It seems odd to give such vague advice on a matter that seems to require bright lines. The clear advice is this: in reality, things are rarely simple because there will be conflicting interests and different perspectives; to ignore that fact would be dangerously naive. That is why we have judges, not just laws. What is important is to listen, to listen carefully enough to really hear, and to take into account the interests of the parties involved. A practical way to do this is to discuss the matter with the stakeholders, which can be done by exploring their motives in the process described in Part 2 of this book. A humble approach to consultation[5] will help make explicit the different interests and the values behind them. Trust and apply the process rather than try to anticipate the outcome.

I remember when I was a young manager in a large corpora-tion, during my annual review, when I complained that I was faced with crossed constraints and conflicting demands from the organization, my boss said to me, 'Saadi, you are a manager; you will be evaluated on the quality of your arbitrations.' The same goes for changemakers. Nothing is easy, but sometimes it is good to have principles and to stand by them. At the very least, you should address issues and clarify for yourself why you have chosen this particular compromise and not another. Would you be willing to make your reasons explicit and public? This is a good test of whether you have given the issue enough thought and work.

A final word: if you took everyone's advice and interests into account, no project would ever happen. At some point you have to make decisions and accept that not everyone will be happy with them. The good thing is that once the change has happened, those who were against it often change their minds.

To conclude: Changing behaviour should be an intervention in people's lives for the better. Determining what is good and what is better is inevitably a political process and should be treated as such. Since the people targeted will also be the actors in the installation, their contribution to the design process is essential. Ethical review, including consultation, is part of the process of deliberately changing behaviour and should be con-sidered at the design stage, when it is still possible to consider different options and ensure that the direction is good. At the very least, the changemaker should be able to make explicit the reasons for his choices and trade-offs. Interventions could use strong measures if those affected agree. All means of intervention should be explicitly considered and discussed for acceptability and proportionality. Those who lose from the change should have their say, be heard and fairly compensated (e.g. better pay, privileged access to services, specific alterna-tive solution).

Of course, discussion does not always solve everything. There are usually objectively conflicting interests, and there will be winners and losers. That is why this is a political issue. Discussion and analysis are a way to find a good compromise, to satisfy as many stakeholders as possible. It is not easy. It takes time. But if you do not try, you will not succeed. One hundred per cent of those who found a compromise have tried to find one. Of course, there are those who tried and did not succeed, but at least they gained experience and knowledge and perhaps moved the system forward a bit. In any case, history shows that the solutions that emerge in the end are better if there was consultation in the process. A formula by my architect friend Volker Hartkopf sums up our approach of ethics: 'You should not work *for* the people, because what you do *for* the people, you do it *to* the people; you should work *with* the people.' Apply the rule locally to find adapted solutions and compromises. The solution may not be perfect, but it will be better than not trying; and you will know why you made the choices you did. Again, trust the process to produce an acceptable outcome.

With this principle of collective intelligence and cooperation in mind, let us examine the various components available to us for intervention. These are the components that society uses to channel behaviour.

5

What makes people behave as they do: installations and their three layers

This chapter introduces installation theory, a powerful framework that enables a systematic analysis of activity. It explains why people do what they do, and describes the three layers of components which combine into 'installations' that channel behaviour. Installation theory also grounds an efficient method to change behaviour, by intervening on these three layers: affordances, embodied competencies, social regulation.

Professor Jones' arrival in Paris

A person's behaviour in a given situation is the result of many factors. Consider, for example, Professor Jones arriving in Paris at the Gare du Nord train station for a meeting at the Paris Institute for Advanced Study in the centre of Paris. How will she get from the station to the Institute? Psychology and economics tell us that the answer depends on Jones' preferences, the cost of the different options, her attitudes regarding more or less sustainable means of transport, her fear of insecurity on public transport, the time taken by each mode of transport, etc. These are indeed factors in economic and psychological theories, but the theory of installation suggests that we should first take a look at the actual conditions and examine what it is that channels the behaviour *in practice*. So let us follow Jones' trajectory of activity.

Rather than inventing her path from scratch, Jones will follow one of several pre-installed channels. There are several options, mainly: walking, renting a public bike, taking bus no. 38, taking the metro line no. 4, taking the fast train line B, or taking a taxi. Since Jones has a suitcase, the bike option is physically impossible; the bike cannot carry a suitcase. Physics is important: only what is physically possible for Jones ('affordances') can occur. This *affordance* factor trumps everything else, because whatever Jones' preferences, however good a cyclist she is, whatever recommendations she may have had, she simply cannot practically choose the bicycle option. That would not work. *The first important factor is environment affordances.*

Then we need to consider Jones' *competencies*. If Jones is familiar with the local public transport system and the geography of the city, it is likely that she will use public transport (including the purchase of the appropriate ticket, a perplexing task for a novice). If she is not familiar with the city, it is likely that Jones will choose to take a taxi, which is easy to find because there is a 'TAXI' sign indicating where to go and get one, and she already knows how to take a taxi. Taking a taxi only requires Jones to state her goal to the driver. *The second important factor is competence.*

However, if Jones' organization has a policy that she should only use public transport on business trips, then she must take the time to learn how to use the Paris public transport system. Alternatively, if the Institute sends a driver to take her directly to the Institute, she is probably going to take that social offer even if she is familiar with the local transport system. The same if the instruction is to take a particular means of transport (e.g. the B line). We see here that a third type of determination is important: the social expectations that one is given; these are very important, trumping the decisions that one would have made with only the first two other types – as long as the final resulting behaviour is compatible with these layers. So, there are cases where you could do it, you know how to do it, but you do not do it because of social pressure and expectations. *Here is the third layer of determination: social regulation.*

All this does not mean that the factors enumerated at the beginning (price, attitudes, etc.) play no role; rather they may be secondary. Furthermore, they might already be included in those three layers of factors above. For instance, Jones' organizational policy for transport ('no taxi, unless no other solution') covers preference for public transport *and* lower cost.

There is more. The human being is a creature that prefers the status quo and often chooses the known solution as the default option, and we have seen in the previous chapters that habit reinforces this channelling. If Jones has learnt how to get from the train station to the Institute by public transit on a previous visit, she will most likely use the same route – unless something prevents her from doing so (such as a transport strike), in which case she will explore the other routes that are available. With each use, the channelled paths are reinforced. But each new episode can still become an opportunity to gain experience and learn new competencies (such as navigating Paris public transport).

The factors we initially considered (Jones' preferences, costs, etc.), while important in principle, are not so important in practice because society has established pathways that people follow. This explains why our description of Jones' trajectory would probably be the same if Jones' gender, age, education, religion, income, etc., were different. This is not to say, again, that these classic (socio-demographic, personality, etc.) variables are irrelevant, just that their effect may be less important than the three types of determination we described (affordances, competencies, social regulation).

Institutions: social regulation

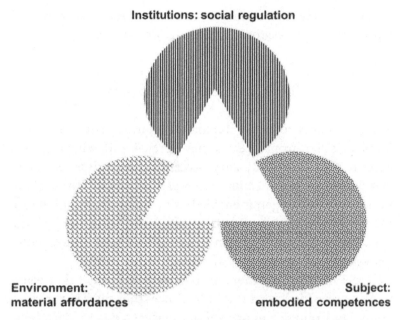

Environment:
material affordances

Subject:
embodied competences

Figure 4 The three layers of components of an installation construct a channelled path (figured by the triangular opening), scaffolding and controlling behaviour.

To conclude, although in theory there are hundreds of variables that could influence the shape of a given behaviour, in practice a behaviour can be channelled rather simply by three main layers of determinants: affordances, embodied competencies and social regulation. These three layers combine to channel behaviour at the point of action. Such a channelling combination of components is an *installation*.

An installation is a specific, local, societal setting where humans are expected to behave in a predictable way. An installation is composed of three combined layers: material affordances of the built environment at the point of action (what is doable), embodied competencies of the actor (the know-how), and social regulation (what is socially expected.)[1]

Interestingly, installations combine the three major assets of humans as a species: tools, knowledge and society.

Tools, knowledge and society

There is not one single biological characteristic in which humans differ from every other species and which would account for our evolutionary success. Nevertheless, our species has developed a *combination of assets* which turned out to be a game-changer; it enabled us to conquer (and plunder) the whole planet in less than 70,000 years, since our species expanded from our African cradle. These assets are tools, knowledge and society.

Tools are a way for humans to make doable what they want to do, to provide the 'can-do' affordances they need in the situation. For example, an axe will make the tree cuttable, a lock will make the door lockable. Tools are mediating structures[2] between the actor and the object that enable the object to have the desired affordance for the equipped human. With the layer of material affordances (objects + tools), installations provide the material conditions necessary to perform the activity.

Knowledge, the second asset, is a way of capitalizing experience, by abstracting it, getting from the particular to the generic, to reuse it in other situations. Building and using knowledge is about exploring, learning, storing, retrieving and reasoning.

To start with, from what happens in succession, we experience consequences; and we bundle together what follows from a specific action in a given situation (e.g. taking the bus provides transport, using the knife cuts the package open). We can then remember this tokenized piece of experience and replay it in the mind. We can compare these tokens and make classes of similar ones (categories), from which we abstract concepts (bus, knife, . . .). Language provides word handles, names to refer to these mental tokens. We learn these names as we learn the categories. So, we learn categories of 'things'. Being able to recognize categories of things is having knowledge. Having knowledge about affordances and about what to do (know-how) and 'what happens if' is a competence. Humans can store this knowledge in their body (memory, acquired reflexes, skills): that is 'embodied competence'. Good installations facilitate the process of learning for their users, by taking particular care of novices as they learn and making the affordances obvious for all, so users can learn in doing and embody the appropriate competencies.

We can then recognize easily that such a thing here and now is an instance of a category, and then apply to it what we know about this category. For example (in London), this big, tall, long red vehicle with many windows and a big number on the front: it is a public bus, and it affords hailing to get transport. Or: this is a packaging, and it affords being cut open; this is a cafeteria, and it affords getting in line to get food. That is powerful because, when I know a category, I can quickly identify an object that belongs to that category with only a few cues. And then (for the Londoner in Paris), this long vehicle with many windows and a big number on the front? – this must be a bus, even though it is not red and very tall. If this is a bus, I can hail it to stop it at a bus stop with the same number on it.

Using only a few cues for decision is called a heuristic,[3] a mechanism we shall see again when we discuss decision processes. A heuristic will identify a category (e.g. bus) from a few cues, and apply the know-how (e.g. hailing) that goes with it. Once we have learned categories, they have become embodied as circuits in our brains. We can re-present these and act on them in thought, just as if they were present to the eye of the mind, consciousness. That is 'reasoning' (i.e. thinking of the bus, how I could use it).

Good installations facilitate with salient cues identification of what this thing here-and-now is, so that the actor can apply her knowledge. Buses are made to be easily identifiable. Their affordances as buses are made obvious – e.g. we put bus stop signs in the locations where buses are stoppable by hailing.

A wonderful property of the tokenization of experience with language is that not only does it enable us to think and reason about objects, but we can also communicate about them. Therefore we can share in a group what would otherwise remain individual experiences, we can learn from others. That is one aspect of the power of living in society; each member can benefit from the experience of the many.

Now, society. Humans use society (the other people) as an orientation system to guide what individuals do. For example, my hailing sign will orient the action of the bus driver, so she stops at the bus stop to take me onboard. The producer of this bag of snacks has signalled me the way to open the packaging with a dotted line. And so on. That social orientation system enables groups to operate as a superorganism with increased agency, through distributed cognition and action, each actor being channelled into doing the right thing in the division of labour. For example, the public transport system moves millions of people every day to where they want to go, at much higher speed and less effort than their individual bodies would, because everyone follows the rules. Tools, knowledge and society are even more powerful when combined, and this is precisely what installations do, with their multilayered structure.

Let us now consider each layer in turn: affordances at the point of action (Chapter 6), embodied competencies (Chapter 7), and social regulation (Chapter 8).

6

The physical layer: affordances of objects at the point of action

This chapter describes the layer of the installation that contains physical components: We examine how its properties contribute to channel behaviour. We define the notion of affordance, what are good affordances, and show how they can be leveraged in installations.

When we orient ourselves during activity, we explore the environment, searching for the relevant 'affordances' available in the context, in order to take the appropriate action. I am hungry, and I think: is there anything edible nearby? I need to open this package: is there anything sharp I can use to cut it open? I am looking for 'affordances' to do what I want to do.

What is an affordance?

The moment you see chairs, tables, books, pianos, apples, you know whether you can carry them, sit on them, eat them, and so on. An object has recognizable properties that allow you to act. These properties are its 'affordances': what you can do with or to it, and what it can do to you. Affordance is about possibility of action. It is the potential for action carried by the object. For example, an apple has the affordance of being eaten. Looking for something sharp to open the package, I look around for the first available object with the satisfying 'cutting' affordance, something that has the potential to cut, e.g. scissors, knife, or even the key in my pocket, to cut the package open.

A good affordance is a possibility of action for the subject, but also – and this is important for our design purpose – a possibility of action that the subject can identify readily.

Action results from a co-operation of the subject with the objects (eating the apple, cutting the package open). Therefore, in our endeavour to design for smooth action, we will have to consider agency on the side of the subject: his competencies (aka skills, ability, know-how, aptitude, effectivity, lata, predispositions, etc., see Chapter 7), and conversely the side of the object. When you sit, the chair does its part of the work by supporting you, with its own agency. Affordances are about the agency of the object.

The affordance of the object will partly depend on the subject: a two-year old child can sit on this highchair, but I cannot because I am too big; this set of stairs may not afford climbing for a disabled person in a wheelchair. This door can be opened or closed by turning the handle, but someone who has two broken arms will not be able to open it. This is a reminder that we should always be aware of who we are designing for, that there will always be special cases, usability issues that we should consider. Still, we can assume that, in general, this door has the affordance to be opened or closed by typical members of a society, with working hands.

The example of the door is an interesting illustration of how affordances can channel trajectories. Doors, stairs, alleys, corridors, roads, are components we install to facilitate and control trajectories in physical space. These physical artefacts determine who can go where and when. They allow and restrict access. They also orient along a given trajectory in space. The same goes for trajectories in general, not just in physical space: these icons on the touch screen can be clicked on and, depending on what I click, my trajectory takes different paths. More generally, affordances create a tree of possible actions and make other actions impossible or difficult to perform. In doing so they drive us towards a specific path. Therefore, we can use affordances in designing intervention to feed-forward the activity in the desired direction. That is typically how passengers are channelled in the airport, for example. Note that, as a result of all these constraints, passengers are empowered to travel safely at high speed to faraway destinations. That is the paradox of channelling: empowering through constraints.

Machines can have powerful and complex affordances. For example, this thermostat provides the affordance of changing the temperature to a given setting: it makes this complex task immediately visible and actionable. Many machines afford doing something by pressing a button. The tumble dryer, like the simple clothes hanger, has the affordance of drying clothes. A good affordance is one that signals what is possible in an obvious way. For example, looking at a door, you should instantly know whether to push or pull to open it. That is why objects often have a handle which naturally indicates where and how to place your hands.

Identifying affordances can require prior knowledge. Humans are good at interpreting simple physical shapes – for example, they can identify accurately if a step is too high for them to climb just by looking at it.[1] For more complicated cases, labels with instructions ('this side up,' 'on/off') or pictures of what to do can be placed on the objects to help the user's orientation. Humans themselves may also display affordances to other humans. Some physical features or attitudes can signal characteristics like strength, potential aggression, or kindness. A cultural system of professional affordances has been developed to display what a given human can do to or with you; e.g. uniforms identify police officers, nurses, soldiers, and other types of professionals.

How affordances scaffold trajectories

In a trajectory, the situation gradually unfolds as the subject progresses in the activity, so the environment provides a constantly changing set of affordances. As you progress along the aisles of a supermarket, a changing array of affordances for shopping will unfold before you. Some products will be more visible, or easier to grab, depending on their position on the shelves. Affordances are used by the subject for the orientation of actions during the course of his or her activity. For example, when peeling vegetables, one constantly monitors which parts of the vegetable remain to be peeled. When the interest of the subject is taken into consideration, this gradual unfolding should be planned in the design of the installation to facilitate orientation and avoid overwhelming the subject with a mass of ambiguous choices.

Still, in many situations, affordances do not automatically emerge for the subject as they progress. In cooking, for example, we alternate between moments in which affordances develop naturally in the flow of activity (such as stirring a mixture until it reaches the expected condition) and moments of orientation in which we must actively seek an affordance (such as looking for an ingredient or utensil). When we build a brick wall, the same: sometimes we stir the cement, and at times we have to go and get more bricks.

To design a good installation, it is necessary to follow the activity of the user, step-by-step, to understand what affordances are needed at each step. A faulty or missing affordance will disrupt the flow of activity and possibly halt it. We can design affordances that naturally lead the subject to the next step, like implementing a walking circuit in an airport, one that gradually leads passengers through corridors, doors, lounges, and counters from the check-in desk to their seat on the plane. The same is true when we design a fluid website. From click to click, the user is guided to the right information.

Along the trajectory, we can force or influence the orientation towards certain variants of behaviour. This can be done in several ways. The simplest (and most efficient) way to channel in a particular direction is to allow only that specific direction of action. On a train, for example, we can open the doors to one side only, so as to let passengers off at the station on the right platform; and, by doing so, prevent passengers from falling on the tracks on the wrong side. We can make it difficult for children to open containers of dangerous chemicals; we can make it impossible for raccoons, ravens and rats to open rubbish bins; we can set up paywalls to access some resources; and so on.

Another way is to make some alternatives more – or less – attractive or salient, e.g. by hiding them from direct view. For example, if you want to avoid snacking, put snacks in the cupboard, keep biscuits in boxes rather than open bowls in full view. Quickly cleaning up graffiti on the walls, and repairing broken windows in an area, avoids signalling the affordance for more graffiti and more broken windows.

Increasing or decreasing cost (physical, emotional, monetary) is also a way to channel the path. For example, according to the economic law of demand, making something more expensive will usually reduce demand.[2] A noisy or uncomfortable environment will discourage people from staying. Many public seatings indoors have been (re)designed specially to prevent homeless people from sleeping in them, i.e. they afford sitting but not lying down. Some fast-food restaurants have designed lighting and colours precisely to avoid people staying too long. Conversely, most cafés and restaurants, to attract clients, strive to offer comfortable environments and they display their dishes and menus to elicit orders. Some airport halls have been specially designed to discourage people from sitting and, instead, channel them into the airport boutiques so they are nudged into shopping. There are also more subtle ways of controlling action by manipulating affordances, such as using fear, which is a powerful emotion. Making a road narrower will slow down drivers; making an object visibly fragile (e.g. glass) will make the user want to handle it with more care.

To design good channelling, we will install in the environment, at the right place in the trajectory, the adequate scaffolding resources, and make their affordance visible. For example, we will place the handle and controls of an industrial press in such a way that it facilitates operation but also keeps the hands away from danger, by forcing the need to have each hand in a handle to unlock the press. Or, as you progress in the cafeteria line, you will be presented in the right order with the tray, and then what you put on it, and so on.

What is a good affordance?

Good affordances display in an obvious manner what they afford. British power sockets indicate whether the socket is on or off; on vehicle dashboards there is an easy-to-read indication of how much fuel is left. What to display, and for what action, is a design issue; e.g. in the case of an electric bicycle, should we display a percentage of charge or the amount of mileage left? If you want to make an affordance very salient, make it sensorily unavoidable: with sound, light, motion. This will attract attention. For example, a flashing light or sound alarm will attract attention if the device fails to satisfy minimal use or reaches a critical threshold. The sensory features that attract our attention are, alas, used and abused by advertisers.

More generally, a good affordance should be interpretable directly by the senses. An analogue representation is faster to interpret than a number. This is why the battery capacity is indicated by bar charts rather than percentage figures, and why vehicle dashboards use dials with hands rather than numerical displays. Indications that require calculation or complex mental operations for the purpose of orienting action are not good ecological interfaces.

If the user is already familiar with a particular type of affordance, changing its appearance for the same function will cause problems. Changing the interface of a computer is problematic because it requires a change of competencies to interpret the affordances. For the same reason, avoiding disorientation of users, some standardization is also needed; e.g. hot-water taps are marked red and cold-water taps are marked blue in many parts of the world. In general, the more salient the affordance and the more immediate the interpretation, the better.

The permanence of affordances

The material layers of an installation have a remarkably useful property: they exist and persist autonomously. Such is not the case for the other two layers, which require the presence of cooperative human beings. For example, if you want to stop vehicles at a level crossing, you can install a traffic warden or a road sign that relies on the driver's ability to interpret it, but the first is demanding in human resource and the second is not fool-proof; on the other hand, installing an automatic level crossing barrier might appear a costly investment but it will be effective 24 hours a day, seven days a week.

To sum up, affordances of objects are what we can do with them, their potential for action. As we move along our trajectory, we are constantly scanning the environment for relevant resources. These resources can be signalled by affordances. A good affordance is one in which this 'can-do' is immediately recognizable and salient to the user in the situation, at the point of action. Affordances both enable and constrain our actions.

They also guide our path, as engaging in the action suggested by the affordance can take us to the next step. Because only what is materially afforded by the material environment can be physically done, and because material objects stand by themselves, affordance is the most powerful and persistent layer of installations for designing interventions.

7

The embodied layer: competencies of the subject

We examine here the components of the installation that are embodied in the subject. The human body has propensities to act, processes that capture and interpret elements of the situation to produce behaviour. I describe some important processes, how they are embodied, how they can be leveraged in installations.

I am looking at the orchard. This tree has yellow fruits I have never seen before. Hmm. What am I going to do? When facing a situation, people address the Fundamental Pragmatic Question, now-what?. They consider what is feasible and then orient into one specific action. What is considered feasible depends on what is *materially* feasible, the affordances that we have just considered in the previous chapter; e.g. whether this fruit is edible, whether this tree is climbable. But the action path resulting from the orientation depends also on the competencies of the subject and his propensity to act in the given circumstance. For example, that yellow fruit on the tree, perhaps it is edible, but I may be unsure of how to eat it (is it ripe? should it be cooked?); or, simply, I may not be hungry.

Another example from genius biologist Jacob von Uexküll.[1] He had brought to the city a smart young man who had never left his remote village and who saw a ladder for the first time. When Uexküll asked him to climb the ladder, the young man said: 'How do you want me to climb? I only see sticks and holes!' But as soon as he had seen another person climbing the ladder, he was able to climb it too.

The ability to perform an action in order to achieve a goal is the *know-how*.[2] The know-how is a competence for interpreting the situation and producing a 'relevant' action, an action that is appropriate to the situation and brings one closer to the goal. For example, as I am waiting at the bus stop to go home, I see the bus arriving: I hail it by raising my arm. That is because *I know* it is the custom here for bus drivers to stop at bus stops, if someone hails them: I have *interpreted* the situation correctly.

'Interpretation' must be understood in the same way musicians interpret a piece of music they read on the score: with both mind and body in a single movement. Not only do I *know* (with my mind) how to raise my hand, but I am also physically *able* (with my arm) to do it. Know-how (some would say 'skill') is a whole-body thing. If I do not have the know-how, I may still act, e.g. driven by my emotions, but my actions may be ineffective; for example, shouting at the bus driver to stop.

The know-how is not *per se* sufficient if it is not well adapted or if the affordance to apply it is absent. In many countries, taxi cabs have a special light that signals if they are available to take customers (e.g. green light is free, red light is not free, unlit means off-duty). Raising one's arm to hail a taxi that is not free has no effect. Tourists and novices, who do not have the local know-how, often hail occupied or off-duty taxis and are disappointed: they do not know how to interpret the situation and act mistakenly. Competence is often the result of learning; it also combines with some innate mechanisms and characteristics of the human body and mind. For instance, in some countries the food recipes use strong chili spice; while the trained locals enjoy it, the occasional visitor might not have the competence to eat this spicy food. Again, the interpretation of affordances, in the embodied mental+physical sense, depends on competencies.

The competencies people have in them include knowledge, and all the propensities, mechanisms and tactics that drive them to act in a given situation, from reflexes, habits and preferences to complex reasoning. This includes all the abilities of our physiological black box, inside the human skin bag. To simplify, I will consider motives, preferences, etc., in the same bag as knowledge, for the practical reason that they all are determinants of action which the subjects carry with them; so, for analysis and design purposes, the subject is the place where we will need to look for them. There are also neuroscientific reasons to avoid making a sharp distinction, but that would be too long to explain in detail here.

Humans are complex organisms; their internal organization contains a vast series of mechanisms that have been selected through biological evolution (e.g. smell, digestion), and others that have been added by education (e.g. literacy, courtesy). The common rationale in this bodily organization is to capitalize and embark on processes that enable the survival and thriving of the organism and of the species: the want-to and the know-how coexist in that same bag of the subject's body. The propensities of the body are a form of competence, they can signal a need and drive the process of satisfying it. For example, feeling hungry when there is a need to refuel the body is putting the subject in a capacity to achieve an important goal: sustaining one's existence.

The metaphor of society as a system might help us to understand the diversity of contents within the human body system. A society is composed of thousands of subsystems that enable its survival and thriving, from roads and harbours to bakeries, police, governments, doctors, couriers, language, tables, chairs, etc. Each category was the result of trials and errors and was finally capitalized; each is in relation to many parts of the system. Some are contradictory (competitors, political parties), some are complementary (buyers and sellers), etc. All these things co-exist in the big bag of 'a society'. So too is the human body, a society of biological cells and organs, a big bag of structures and processes that enable the organism as whole to thrive in its environment, a bag of tricks, a toolbox, of which the rationale is biological rather than logical. As humans themselves are an essential component of the installations, the changemaker must have some understandings of what competencies are, where they come from, and how they can be learned and modified.

In what follows, I will describe some important aspects of this bodily society of cells. This cannot be exhaustive and looks a bit of a laundry list: just as for describing the organs of the human body, it is difficult to organize them in a logical order – because the system was not *designed* with a logical order. I am just trying to describe here what appeared to me the most relevant contents of this big bag of organs and processes in the perspective of behavioural production and change.

How evolution, culture and education filled the bag of tricks of the human body

The medium where competencies are embodied, the human body, carries in itself certain predispositions that orient its interpretation of the situation. Some predispositions come from the history of our species, they are innate and universal. Other dispositions are acquired through individual and social experience. All these combine to produce the 'competencies', which are the ability to perform behaviours adapted to a situation, from perception to relevant action. For example, we combine our visual predisposition to see small objects with our school education into 'literacy,' the know-how of reading.

Humans have some innate competencies that are universal across cultures. We all start life with a human body that has similar specific biological predispositions (e.g. vision). Evolution has profoundly marked our species, which for millennia lived as hunting-gathering tribes. Primates, our zoological order, appeared over 55 million years ago, and sedentary Neolithic was only 12,000 years ago, so our history as 'civilized' human beings is very recent and did not have much time to impact our physiology. If all humankind history were a day, the beginning of the Neolithic period would correspond to approximately one minute before midnight. So, most of our innate competencies are the ones selected to be a fit, social, tribal hunter-gatherer rather than a civilized citizen of large-scale societies. In many aspects we are close to our cousins the other great apes, chimpanzees or ourang outangs, because we are biologically very similar.

Then people living in similar conditions, in the same environment, tend to have similar experiences, and therefore to develop similar dispositions and propensities. That is why we talk about 'habitus' and 'culture'. Cultural traits are not universals, but they are shared by the members of a community. There are still discussions among specialists about which cognitive propensities are universals. Since all human cultures share some similarities, it is difficult to distinguish firmly between innate and acquired, between predispositions and dispositions: for example, as mentioned earlier in relation to feral children, bipedal walk and language are universal among humans, but have to be acquired.

Beyond cultural traits, individuals develop their own specific 'personality', a combination of cognitive style and generic ways of approaching situations, like psychological defence mechanisms, or relational style (e.g. extrovert). Throughout life, each person develops individual dispositions, tastes, habits, and preferences for certain colours, foods, smells, activities, people, etc. Personality is often grounded in what produced good or bad results in their experience, on top of what was encouraged and rewarded/punished in their local culture, social class, education, age group, etc. For example, in some countries, females are encouraged to be cooperative, while males are encouraged to be competitive, but individual diversity persists beyond that conditioning. Anyway, we humans are educable. This educability is my main source of hope as a social scientist, considering the rest of what we know about humans.

When we attempt to change the installation, we will take advantage of this educability to edit competencies, by combining dispositions and experience. For example, we can educate citizens to take buses, or use less water. We can also leverage existing dispositions; e.g. we can play on competitiveness, sexual drive or risk aversion. A smart changemaker will also consider local cultural specificities as the background in which installations will operate.

Propensities and dispositions

There are diverse types of propensities and dispositions. They have been called by many names: 'motives', 'preferences', 'biases', 'heuristics', etc. They can be innate, acquired, often a combination of both; they can be permanent or situational.

As hinted above, a lot of what we are comes from the history of our species, of which our current bodies and minds are a result. Some cognitive characteristics are deeply integrated in human physiology. For example, we instinctively tend to turn our attention to noise and movement, our interest is naturally caught by some objects, features or events (e.g. babies, snakes, violence, some sexual features). Innate characteristics also include limitations. For example, humans hardly hold more than seven elements simultaneously in short-term memory.[3] That is why, when you are introduced to many people at the same time, it is so difficult to remember all their names. All humans share these limitations and 'biases'.

With other primates and many animals we share the basic survival need to maintain our own body alive by breathing, avoiding harm, consuming food, maintaining our internal temperature, etc. We also need to raise our offspring, who require care for longer than in most other species, care for which we adults cooperate. Beyond childcare, our cooperation enables us to accomplish tasks beyond the strength and cognitive abilities of a single individual. For example, together we can carry heavy weight, build large houses. Because cooperation makes us more efficient, in the course of evolution, among groups, those who were cooperative (e.g. in hunting or fighting) survived better and reproduced more; over millennia of group selection this made humans what they are now: a sociable and cooperative species. As language facilitates cooperation, and vice versa, in a virtuous loop, we humans became particularly good at language – and at cooperation. Humans are a very social and talkative species by nature; we like stories, we like company.

The main motives relate to basic needs for the survival of the species mentioned above (breathing, etc.), including reproduction and sociability. Then, people satisfy these basic motives directly (e.g. eating) but also strategically with instrumental activities (e.g. foraging). The latter are so efficient as a proxy to satisfying various needs that they are motives of their own, such as protection (which makes us cautious), exploration (to learn useful things), and acquisition of resources (material, social, informational). Among those motives that drive useful behaviours are competition, defending our territory, making friends, curiosity, getting high social positions (ambition), having a good appearance, exchanging information (e.g. gossip). Among those again seems to be a drive for foraging (shopping!) which our past as hunters-gatherers may explain, and perhaps a generic productive drive coming with our tool savviness. This list is non exhaustive. For instance, people seem to be motivated by listening to music, walking in nature, acting in groups, having pets, and collecting (useless) items.

Some predispositions are not motives *per se*, but rather an automatic form of reaction, akin to innate reflexes to specific types of stimulation – e.g. we will automatically protect our body against fast-moving objects coming our way. We also automatically experience specific emotions in certain circumstances, like parental love or sexual arousal. These emotions are connected to the subjective experience of being motivated.

Those propensities that we usually find in the bag of predispositions of the human body have stayed there because the behaviours they trigger are beneficial at least in some specific cases and are automatically elicited, like aggressiveness when subject to frustration or aggression. Those motives that set us in motion in case of need, or opportunity, or as a reaction to situation, are all shortcuts of generic strategies to address a behavioural problem, internal (e.g. lack of nutrients) or external (e.g. resource opportunity or danger).

Often, the drive to act is some transformation of an innate basic motive (instinct) by the local culture, sometimes in such a way that the underlying instinct is difficult to identify – for instance, in artistic or aesthetic activities. This may be a problem for psychologists, but the difference does not matter much for the changemaker. Hence, we will consider one single bag, with the propensities and agency the subject carries in her body (want-to, know-how).

Biases, heuristics and the default mode

Now a word about 'biases'. Compared to 'logical reasoning', the way humans actually behave shows differences, which economists and some psychologists called biases, or heuristics. These are ways of processing information, and making choices, in apparently irrational ways. Rather than a lengthy list of sometimes obscure definitions, let us look at the principles at work, which will also facilitate designing interventions.

Usually, the response to the now-what? need not necessarily be the best, because taking the time and effort to find a best response is costly and could take forever (how are we sure that is indeed the best?). The response just needs to be good enough. And the now-what? needs to be answered *now*; hesitation could make us lose the opportunity. In that realistic context, humans have developed strategies and shortcuts that usually work *well enough* to ensure sufficient satisfaction and minimize risk. For example, when choosing a product, I will rely on the brand; on choosing which waiting line at the cashier, I will go for the shortest; on picking a hotel I will rely on the reviews; and so on. The general idea is to decide by using only a fraction of the information available, or to explore only a specific set of possibilities; this cut-corner approach is called a heuristic. I can do this because I have the competence to recognize a category, e.g. 'waiting line', and the know-how that the shorter the line the shorter the wait; so this visible cue (length of line) is a short-cut to guide my choice.

By nature, heuristics tend to consider some aspects of the situation or alternatives more than others, therefore they are 'biased'. For example, there is a preference for immediate present rewards over future rewards ('future discounting bias'), a preference for attributing 'causes' to other people rather than to circumstances ('fundamental attribution bias'), a preference for maintaining the current solution as the default and basis for comparison ('status quo bias'), and so on.

So, heuristics come from the tendency of humans to allocate a minimal effort of computation to orientation, to the point that humans have been called 'cognitive misers'. This is perfectly understandable and, in a way, functionally rational in the orientation process, since considering alternatives and evaluating them in detail takes time and resources. The brain is not a muscle, but it consumes a lot of energy (20% of the whole body). Also, thought and attention are limited resources. While the brain is focused on a complex evaluation, it cannot attend to other tasks. For example, in the line at the cafeteria, when I hesitate between different dishes, I will probably stop in front of the dishes to consider the options because I need time to think. I cannot do anything else while I am thinking carefully. Sometimes I must even stop moving. And at some point, I will feel the pressure from other people waiting in the queue behind me.

We face hundreds of orientation episodes every day. If at every single one we were to consider the situation anew, and consider it in detail, life would be impossibly slow (especially if everyone did so). Consider my stopping in the cafeteria queue to think in depth about whether I should choose the healthy broccoli or the tasty French fries. Even if it takes only three seconds (a usual orientation time) to think at each such orientation (for choosing dessert, drinks; finding a table . . .), this would be a serious slowdown. In fact, such systematic but slow decision-making was not the best strategy for survival for our hunter-gatherer ancestors, who were confronted with the rapid pace of life in the wild: is this noise in the bush a predator that can kill me, or some prey I could catch? Should I, right now, flee or attack? Is that raised hand a gesture of threat or friendship? Some now-what? questions require an immediate response. Many smart but slow individuals ended up dead. It turns out that we inherited a tendency to think fast, but not necessarily deeply,[4] and that we are spontaneously driven by emotions rather than reason. (That is, by the way, why you should never take an important decision on a whim, and without having slept on it.)

Human beings' emotional and core cognitive processes are adapted to the fundamental pragmatic question, now-what? But this question is local – it is only about *here* and *now* – so there are limitations in time and space in the scope of our cognitive competencies. We tend to be ill-equipped to consider the future (beyond *now*) and externalities (beyond *here*). That is why we need regulations that bring these far- and long-ranging factors into the 'here and now' orientation. That is precisely what society does with institutions which prevent us from creating negative externalities ('do not pollute') and avoid jeopardizing the future ('do not smoke').

In orientation, a very powerful heuristic is the 'default choice'. The default choice is to use a response to the now-what? that appears satisficing and does not require calculation or speculation. Typically, re-using the same behaviour that has worked previously in similar circumstances will do. For example, I use the same route to travel from home to work; I always go to the same dentist, I keep my account in the same bank, I always start shaving with the same cheek. That is why *habits* are so powerful: they provide a good, proven, default option. For example, we tend to buy again the same products that we found satisfactory: 'I know the product' is the first cause for buying it (again). Default options are economical because they hardly require any mental effort and offer a safe outcome.

When an option is presented as something that other people do in similar circumstances, this may also appear as a good answer to the now-what? Again, this spares the burden of thorough exploration to solve the now-what? if you trust other people's choice. That is a reason why social norms are so efficient; that is also why imitation of, or advice by, trusted people works well. That is why, for example, the 'testimonials' of famous people, or the reviews by other consumers, influence our buying behaviour.

Then there are other possible economies in mental process-ing: we tend to use the most available information, that is the one that is most visible (salience) or accessible in memory (recency) or the easiest to understand (e.g. analogue rather than symbolic: a bar graph, a colour code, are faster to decode than a table of figures). All these require less mental work. The easiest information to access is that which is present to the senses at the point of action; even easier than searching in memory. That is why, when they search for something, people first scan the environment for affordances, or for guidelines, panning their heads left and right rather than searching in their memory where they saw the object the last time.

Considering the above, if we wish to channel behaviour, we should make the answer to the now-what? obvious, and with very few options (ideally, only one stands out). Presenting, in succession, a simple sequence of actions to do is the best because it has the form that responds to the problem of activity, which is in practice a sequence of now-what?: 'What do I do now? And then now? And then now?' And so on. At each step, the subject should be presented with the readymade responses that society has come up with, responses that include prescriptions for action. That is typically what good installations do.

Learning new behaviours

When we want to teach people different behaviours, it is important to know how people learn new behaviours and/or change their current habits. There are many ways to learn, but they all result in the same: changing durably the way our body cells are connected into operational circuits. Thought is activation of neuronal circuits in the brain; memory is a favoured circuit between neurons in the brain.

The generic principle by which we learn from experience is called the law of effect.[5] That is how we learn about consequences ('if this, then that'). Humans learn by associating in their memory what they perceived together (e.g. the smell of the horse and the sight of the horse); but the law of effect is more than that, it records a sense of temporal succession and a hint of causality. We associate our experience (of perception and action) with the effect it had, e.g. positive or negative outcome, and the emotions that go with it. This is especially useful for learning about action and the effect it has. What had positive effect we tend to do again in similar circumstances, what had negative effect we tend to avoid doing again.

This law of effect can be used in conditioning, with punishment and reward; more generally it is at the basis of much of our behavioural learning. I mentioned earlier how tastes can be acquired through experience, with the example of vanilla-flavoured baby milk formula. Most culturally acquired behaviours are behaviours that were learned in a social context where they were elicited and then rewarded, or when failing to perform them was punished. And, often, both reward for compliance *and* punishment for non-compliance – e.g. rules of politeness, clothing styles.

Here is how experience transforms into physiological structures. As we act, we connect perception of a given situation to our actions; this activates corresponding structures in our brain. This experience creates a lasting connection between these co-activated structures. What has been activated together once will be activated together more readily later. To simplify, the more used a circuit is, the more fluid it becomes, the most it will tend to be reactivated in similar circumstances, in the way that a threaded path in the forest attracts the hikers' walk.

We see this phenomenon at work in the association of ideas, and in acquired reflexes, but it also works more generally for any ideas and actions. For example, experience will associate the affordance of the sharp edge and the experience of the cut, the perception of the flame and the experience of the burn, the practice of the bus and the idea of transportation. So, when one thing is perceived, the connected stuff is evoked. This goes both ways: if I see the sharp edge, I think of the cut and I am weary. Conversely if I think of the cut, for example if I need to cut something, this will evoke the sharp edge and therefore I will be looking for a sharp edge.

Experience is not just the connection of a chain of events: it is also coloured with the emotional aspects we experience as we act. Emotions are fully part of the memory of the action; as we act the whole experience is cropped as it is connected, in a single bundle. I missed the train and felt frustrated and angry, I climbed the mountain and at the top I felt exhausted but exhilarated: these emotions will stick with the recall of the event in my memory.

Things evoke positive feelings if they have been connected with pleasure in previous experience (e.g. for many of us, chocolate). The evocation can also be negative if some pain or dissatisfaction was the outcome of a previous interaction (e.g. wasp). Therefore, in the process of orientation, at the point of action, when the subject considers several possible courses for action, the associated emotions will be evoked. Then, one alternative may come with positive accents, while another may have negative accents. And that will of course influence the orientation. For example, here I am at the supermarket, choosing between various brands of plastic garbage bags. In my experience, the brand I bought last time was not robust, it leaked; I had to clean the kitchen floor and the stinking garbage can, which was an unpleasant experience. Therefore I pick another brand. Now I am at the cafeteria (again!); as I must choose between various dishes, I see the choice today is French fries or broccoli. In my experience, the fries tasted good, but the broccoli did not. I am inclined to go for the fries. More generally, the mere fact of achieving your goal brings satisfaction, therefore a successful trajectory, and its components, will be connoted with that positive halo. Here we recognize how the law of effect induces learning, and the emotional mechanism behind it. The long-lasting effect of trauma shows how deep and strong the impact of experience can be. The stronger the emotion, the deeper the impact; and probably the longer the acquired disposition can last.

Because our nervous system is inside our body, we can also activate its circuits without external input (perception) or output (action). We can 'think': we can consider different paths of action, simulate experience in our mind, and 'make decisions' in light of future outcome (the goal), especially if we already know a path to this goal. Then, of course, it will be easier to activate the neural circuits that correspond to that path and are fluid and well threaded, and if they have a positive connotation. Positive experience of an action for a given purpose is a facilitator of thought of performance of the same action for similar purpose later. That is why we tend to buy again the same foods. That also explains why criminals and other deviants find it easier to perform forbidden behaviour (such as stealing, killing) after they have already done it once, and the more they've done it, the easier it is – if they got away with it.[6]

What goes for learning what-to-do also goes for learning what *not* to do. We learn to avoid some situations, and that learning is intense and durable. For instance, if you get sick after eating a specific food, you will be disgusted by this food for a long time. That is why patients who get aggressive chemotherapy (which makes you sick) are told to eat unusual foods, to avoid getting disgusted by their usual food, which their body, following the law of effect, might mistakenly associate as the cause of feeling sick. If you get punished, you are likely not to reiterate.

We can also learn to resist and fight. The body learns not only with the neurons of the brain, but with other types of cells too; e.g. immunity to disease is the result of experience. Since a substantial amount of behaviour will happen in channelled mode, where the 'neural attractors' of these well-trodden circuits will operate, our goal as changemakers is to foster the creation of the proper circuits, new attractors which will reinforce through practice. So, for novices the first exposure is critical; and for the others we should create opportunities for change, where they can positively experience the practice we want to foster.

Direct lived experience is the most powerful and lasting, because it activates a lot of different subsystems of perception and action circuits: it is 'multimodal'. This lived experience activates circuits of all our senses, vision, hearing, touch, taste, smell, balance, but also proprioception (joints and muscles) and various other inner physiological systems. It is rich in emotions. It is also connected as a time sequence that links it to our sense of being, our motives, and so on. It feels 'real', and often intense.

But there are many other ways by which humans learn. We can also learn by indirect experience, watching others doing ('social learning').[7] We are avid watchers of such social learning experiences where we can see what happens without taking the risk of trying ourselves. Those of our ancestors who were good at that survived better. That is probably why we are so fascinated when looking at accidents, competitions or success. Indeed, when we watch someone acting, the very act of presenting the action in our brain activates similar circuits ('mirror neuron circuits')[8] and this facilitates our social learning. This is especially relevant for behaviours we learn for the first time. For example, I see, lying wounded on the pavement, this fallen cyclist who was not wearing a helmet. This shocking experience will make me avoid riding without a helmet – at least for some time.

We can also learn from abstract representation, through language, for example, or even from imagination. Then the circuits of perception and action are evoked and re-enacted by some description, and emotions as well. I hear that my colleague was the victim of a scam by opening an email, and this makes me careful. My friend tells me that this bakery is excellent, and I will go and buy bread there. Indirect learning, though, is not as powerful and enduring as direct experience. That is why students forget the lessons they did not have the opportunity to apply in practice, and why your children and friends still make the mistakes about which you warned them. And that is why trying to persuade people to do something with only abstract arguments usually does not have much impact on their actual behaviour (as we will see below with Lewin's classic experiment on offal).

Some propensities the changemaker can leverage.

Competencies, these characteristics of the human material, are for the changemaker components to leverage when designing installations. By playing with these competencies we can frame the process of orientation and drive the subject into taking one or the other course of action. The list of competencies that humans have or can learn is endless, since we are educable. I will now give a (non-exhaustive) list of especially interesting propensities of the human material that are used in installations. Some are leveraging the specific strategies of humans to address the now-what?: relying on tools, knowledge and fellow humans. Others are more connected to generic basic strategies: competition, risk avoidance, motivation.

Tool use

Humans have hands with opposing thumbs that enable them to manipulate objects and use tools skilfully. The use of tools was a great advantage during evolution. The most able with tools had more survival and reproductive success; humans became a species very apt at using tools, but also one that tends to rely on tools. Humans tend to go around carrying tools all the time, in pockets and bags. Even Ötzi, the neolithic man who died 5,300 years ago and whose corpse was found mummified in excellent state of conservation in the Alps, carried a backpack.

When confronted with a problem, one of the first spontaneous reactions of the human being is to scan the environment for objects that could be used as tools to address the situation. This may seem natural to us, but this 'looking out for tools' when confronted with a problem is not what other animals do. This is used in installations: because in situations humans will be looking for such affordances, making available a tool *with specific affordances* facilitates funnelling the action. Humans will naturally scan the environment, literally looking for something with the right affordance in the installation. Make salient that affordance that will take them to what you want to be their next step, and they are likely to use it. Affordances are bait for action.

Knowledge

Another human propensity when addressing the now-what? is to use knowledge. Knowledge is capitalized experience, from self or others. There are several ways to use knowledge. It can provide an immediate solution we know as satisficing, validated by personal experience (e.g. habit, default option). It can suggest a possibly good solution coming from indirect experience (e.g. advice, common knowledge). It can be used to combine other related knowledge to produce a possibly good solution (reasoning). Knowledge can be injected into the orientation process at these three levels.

Default

I have already mentioned the default solution, the powerful heuristic that saves the mental effort of evaluating solutions other than the most salient one when it is presented as a valid option. The appeal of the default option is also at work in the status quo bias, the preference for not changing the current situation or practice. Designing for default is an important tool for behavioural intervention. However, while designing for default can be straightforward when it comes to presenting a box to tick or an opt-out option on a form, it can be more difficult to implement for actions in the physical world.

Ideally, the first exposure to the action should be correct and successful. This means that installations should be very well designed for beginners, to ensure that they get it right the first time; for example, by offering a simple track for beginners, even if that simple track does not include all the possibilities and subtleties of the whole installation. Or installations should facilitate learning. Consider the design of a dance hall. There is space on the sides for those who are unsure of how to do it, so they can watch and learn until they can act on their own, often after a period of supervised trial. In many venues you will find some form of receptionist or other type of attendant to guide you through the steps.

Ready-made thought: social representations

In a situation, we draw heuristics from our embodied library of cognitive tools (or 'mediating structures') that culture has prepared for us. For example, how to recognize and hail a taxi, how to behave at a wedding, and many other things. This is how we cognitive misers decipher and interpret situations without constantly making complex assessments and reinventing the wheel. Interestingly, these ready-made interpretations depend on culture; and while the local person will immediately know what to do, the stranger may not have the appropriate ones (remember the taxi example).

These ready-made answers exist in society in the form of ready-made thoughts for most objects. They describe 'types' of objects and what specific behaviour we can expect from them. For example: 'the fireman', 'the teacher', 'the mother', 'the singer', 'the socialite'. More generally, every object that has a name in a language also has a 'social representation' in the population that uses that language. The social representation[9] is the common-sense description of how to recognize the object in question, what to expect from it, how to use it: 'a table', 'a prison', 'diarrhoea', etc. This ready-made thought (found in dictionaries and encyclopaedias) offers an answer to the now-what?. It provides a cultural shortcut from perception to action; it avoids processing all the information and allows only a small part of the available information to be used. For example, I see 'a shop'; I immediately understand that what is on display can be obtained for money. I see fruit in an orchard, I understand that I can only have it if the owner gives me permission.

Social representations are the result of such objects having been part of installations for a long time, so that the embodied competencies that go with them have permeated society and become part of culture. Amazingly, each of us has embodied a vast encyclopaedia of these social representations. We all know what a bus is, what a chair is, what a policeman is, what a railway station is, and a thousand other things, including such complex things as a hospital, an election, a funeral. We even know phenomena that we have never experienced, such as an earthquake, a tsunami and a space station. We have learned about them through practice, observation or communication.

In fact, one of the aims of media campaigns is precisely to build or edit social representations in the hope that this ready-made thought will guide people's behaviour. The plasticity of human beings is amazing, and what their culture can make them believe is normal behaviour can be surprising. It is only when we travel that we realize that what seems 'normal' in one place may not be so in another. When I moved to the UK I was surprised by the local design of windows (sashes, casement windows) which cannot be cleaned from the inside only, because they cannot be opened all the way. Their outside can only be cleaned from outside. This makes it difficult to clean windows above ground level. The British use giant poles that are operated from the ground, poles that have a sponge at the end and a hose that constantly feeds water to the sponge. Or they use acrobatic window cleaners. Every culture has its peculiar installations, and the natives adapt.

Finally, if there is no ready-made or obvious answer, an easy option (the status quo) is to make no decision and continue on the current trajectory. This is also a (common) form of default. For example, when we have to renew a contract (e.g. bank, insurance) or a product, and after hesitating between several options, we simply keep the old one and postpone the decision to 'later'. Or we keep our windows dirty unless we have acrobatic skills and long poles.

Reasoning

If there is no common-sense answer to the now-what?, and we are under pressure to act, we can combine other knowledge and simulate what might be a possible solution. This is reasoning, an approach used when there is no simpler way. We can act out hypothetical situations in the theatre of our mind, such as possible futures, and simulate what we would do in those hypothetical situations. We can make plans, we become strategic: securing resources, preventing dangers. We can understand and imagine the possible negative consequences of our behaviour (in the future, for others, . . .), we can agree to make efforts to minimize such negative effects. As we seek relevant information and are open to different inputs, this openness can be used to persuade people to adopt a new behaviour.

The installation can provide information that will help to orient the subject in the desired direction. For example, we can display knowledge about the product on labels and packaging. That is the classic informative approach; it is more likely to be effective if it is provided at the point of action. Note, however, that there is hardly anything like pure rational thinking: emotions and social influences are interwoven with these thought processes. In the complex system that is my body, many circuits are activated simultaneously. There are over ten billion neurons in my brain alone. When choosing between chips and broccoli, I might also consider the price, the quantity, the nutritional value, my level of hunger, my diet, what my neighbours are choosing, and so on. Then, depending on how the 'current conditions' are presented to me, some aspects might be more salient than others, and activate circuits that contribute to my orientation.

Logical reasoning might prevail, but it does not always. The idea proposed by some economists that people behave as 'rational agents' is wrong. For example, yesterday my colleague wrote an angry email out of frustration – even though he knew that sending it would make things worse. And there are, according to paternity tests, some one per cent of children born out of 'extra-conjugal copulation' (adultery or equivalent)[10] – even though the biological parents knew that following their instincts and emotions against social rules can create complicated situations.

Activity is not the product of a rational agent, perhaps limited by some 'biases'. Rather, it is the trajectory of an intelligent human body, driven by motives, informed by experience and channelled by social institutions, opportunistically exploiting the given conditions to achieve its goals. Our purpose, therefore, is not to inform rational agents in order to enable them to make decisions that maximize their interests. Rather, it is to provide the material, mental and social conditions that enable and channel subjects to achieve satisfaction – while minimizing the negative externalities of their behaviour.

The art of the changemaker will be to select and make more salient the positive aspects of those components that will channel behaviour in the desired direction, and the negative aspects of other trajectories; and to evoke the emotions that will facilitate the target behaviour. This is what good salespeople do (as well as tricksters and illusionists): they focus their audience's attention on the aspects of the situation that serve their purpose and hide the others.

The less time I have to orient myself, the more I will rely on proven solutions. And the more my mind is occupied with attending to other things, the more I will rely on proven solutions because my mental processing capacity is limited. So, in practice, I will prefer solutions that require little processing, even more when I have little time or mental capacity. Especially when the problem is complex: it is more difficult to choose from thirty flavours of ice cream than from three.

The implication of this is that if you put people under time pressure, they will make choices without much thought, and will be inclined to take the option offered. This is pretty much what salespeople do when they tell you that this offer is only valid for a short time, and you should decide right now. It works, but this technique should only be used when you have a solid ethical justification.

Conversely, if we want people to decide rationally, or to deviate from the default option, we should give them time and space to consider the new option, an approach called 'boosting', and this new option should then be presented with arguments suggesting that this new course of action will satisfy better than the current default course of action, to feed reasoning.

Dissonance

The discomfort of holding two conflicting beliefs, values or attitudes is called dissonance. For example, the discrepancy between what we believe is right and what we actually do. Dissonance is uncomfortable because it blocks the response to the now-what? by suggesting competing alternatives rather than an easy path. People do not like dissonance. Dissonance suggests either that you are doing something wrong, or that your knowledge system is not consistent and adapted to reality. Either way, it means that you cannot trust yourself, and that is an uncomfortable feeling. In such situations people change their practice or (which is often easier) they change their beliefs. They prefer to feel consistent. For example, suppose I have harmed a person: I am likely to tell myself that the person is bad, so they deserve it; this avoids feeling contradiction and guilt. Suppose I take drugs: I can either stop, or convince myself that it is not such a bad behaviour. In both cases I am reducing dissonance, but the second way is easier.

The drive to reduce dissonance can be harnessed. The first way is to make people believe something and hope that they will change their practice accordingly. This is what communication campaigns do, and they rarely work. Another way, counterintuitively, is to make people do something and make them aware of it so that they align their beliefs with their actions. For example, if you want someone to like you, ask them for help. If they have helped you and you have thanked them, they will usually like you more and help you again, because you usually help people you like. So, if they have helped you, you must be likeable.

Dissonance can arise from a gap between intention and behaviour. People know what's right, but they don't do it. For example, they know they should use reusable items instead of disposable ones (e.g. cups, batteries). In such cases, we can give them a low-risk, low-cost, no-obligation first experience of a different way of doing things. For example, by offering a free trial – a classic commercial trick. Then, since even a free trial can be seen as useless ('why? I already have something that works!'), we may need to use an incentive. Social influence ('the other members of your community are doing it!') is one such incentive. If the experience of this first attempt at a new behaviour is positive, e.g. bringing benefit and possibly social recognition, the new behaviour is likely to be adopted. Unfortunately, this forced test is also the technique used by gangs to get the newcomer to engage in illegal behaviour.

Persuasion and influence

Experts distinguish between 'persuasion' and 'influence' approaches. Persuasion is the use of rational arguments in the orientation process in the hope that the subject will consciously decide that one option is better for rational reasons and choose that option. For example, I will choose the vegetarian option, or use public transport rather than my own car, because I have been persuaded by scientific arguments that this is better for the planet. Influence,[11] on the other hand, is about using heuristics, dissonance and social pressure: it is about the process of orientation rather than the content of the option chosen. For example, I will buy this particular brand of product because I see this famous person using it. As we will see in the next chapter, this propensity can be exploited by others.

Persuasion uses rational arguments or heuristics to change a person's attitudes and representations about something, leading them to adopt the target behaviour of their own volition; the source should be trusted as knowledgeable. Influence, on the other hand, often plays on consistency to get a person to engage in the target behaviour. The target's motive is to appear consistent, and this is exploited. A classic example: beggars and crooks will often approach you on the street and ask you a simple question ('What time is it?' 'Do you speak English?'). If you respond positively to their first request, you will be more likely to respond positively to their next request (money). You have already given them something (time, attention); you are now committed to helping them: why not be consistent and give them a little more? This is called the 'foot in the door' technique, where you make a small request and then ask for something bigger. This is another example of other people taking advantage of the target's social and consistency propensities.

Sociability

Sociability is essential to human beings. It is an embodied propensity. Psychological experiments and neuroscience show that people feel emotionally rewarded when they engage in altruistic behaviour; they experience the 'warm glow'. For example, you may feel a warm glow when you give a gift to someone or give alms to a beggar. More generally, we enjoy doing things together, participating in groups. The moments we remember most fondly are usually social moments. We may even, in extreme cases, sacrifice ourselves for the group.

What people want more than anything is to belong, to feel part of a community that recognizes them. Providing social recognition (e.g. membership, approval) is a huge incentive. People want to signal that they belong to their community in order to be recognized and to be given status. They will go to astonishing lengths for this 'signalling'. For example, people will follow the dress code of their group. They will spend enormous amounts of money to obtain items that signal their position in the group ('positional goods'): expensive vehicles, jewellery, etc. This is why brand logos are so popular.

Observing football fans gives a measure of how excessive this drive to belong can be, how deeply ingrained it is in our tribal ape nature, and how stupid and possibly dangerous people can become under its influence. Of course, the changemaker can harness this powerful drive; please use moderation.

Cooperation

Cooperation (especially with one's own group) is natural to us, and so in a given situation people will spontaneously tend to see what others are doing and to follow what seems to be the group norm, e.g. by asking or imitating. Volunteering for charities and non-profits, or helping after disasters, are examples. Ask people to help and you will not usually be disappointed. Society encourages this drive and rewards cooperation with public recognition and praise. It facilitates the visibility of 'good' examples; conversely, society teaches that 'bad' behaviour will be rebuked with public blame and punishment.

More generally, the social drive in its many aspects is an extremely powerful lever on behaviour and, while society uses it massively, it is usually under-used in professional installation design. More on this in the next chapter.

Risk avoidance

When it comes to the now-what?, a common human tendency is to avoid risk. In the ecological setting of a hunter-gatherer, failing to gain a resource we do not yet have can be frustrating, but losing one we do have can be disastrous. This risk may explain why people usually tend to fear loss more than they value gain. Also, because the status quo is something we know is viable, it is less risky to do nothing and stay in our current 'default' situation (the status quo) than to take action that involves the risk of loss, not to mention the effort of change. Change involves transaction costs (finding information, training on the new system);[12] it also involves unknown risks.

In practice, people often stick with sub-optimal choices: for example, they rarely change banks, jobs or countries, or sell their shares even if they fall in value. Of course, individuals may be more or less risk-averse depending on their own history, but there is a general human tendency to avoid risk. This conservative principle extends to the future: we will tend to prefer a smaller certain gain now to a larger one in the future, because the future means uncertainty and risk. Of course, this should not logically hold if the future were certain, as it is presented in economic games: 'Would you rather get $10 now or $12 in 6 months?' In practice, however, most participants in these experiments choose $10 now.

The guarantee of some authority that the 'good' option is safe may be enough to overcome the risk of change. Publishing other users' ratings can also work well, but then there are the classic caveats about using ratings. Now, be aware that, while people often tend to be risk averse, they may also be willing to take risks in specific circumstances. So many people play the lottery! Attitudes towards risk is one more of these opposite pairs of propensities human beings all have.

Competition

Humans are cooperative, but they are also competitive by nature. Competition tends to develop competencies that are positive for the individual and possibly for the group as a whole (strength, skill, intelligence, etc.). Throughout evolution, individuals who were more successful in accessing and using resources than their peers often survived better. And they reproduced better, so this was passed on. This natural competitive drive can be seen in sport and many other areas.

Competition and cooperation are somewhat antagonistic. But they coexist in human beings, as do other pairs of antagonistic drives (aggression and care, fear and exploration, risk aversion and risk taking, etc.) The way human beings deal with these two specific antagonistic drives (competition and cooperation) is to create hierarchies. In hierarchies, competition organizes individuals within the group and thus remains compatible with cooperation within the group. Hierarchies create a permanent power structure in the group that facilitates decision-making and coordinated action. Competition also has a dark side, creating inequality, frustration and antagonism, so societies create safeguards against its excesses.

Gamification is one way of harnessing the competitive drive of users. Gamification does not have to be about competing against someone else, it can be about competing against a benchmark or against one's own past performance. Allow people to measure their performance and give them feedback on their level. Many 'quantified self' devices, such as smartwatches that track your performance and, of course, all competitions, tap into this motive.

Motivation

Finally, since action is driven by the motive, reminding the subject of the motive ('motivation') during action is effective in increasing effort. This is often done by displaying pictures of the goal, success or reward (e.g. in gyms, pictures of fit stars and trophies; in many organizations, pictures of past or present leaders).

Do changemakers need extensive psychological knowledge?

One might wonder whether it is necessary to have extensive knowledge of psychology in order to design installations. Does the changemaker need to know all the human heuristics, motives, etc.? Well, yes and no. Extended psychological knowledge can be useful, and calling the help of an expert will usually provide it. Nevertheless, regarding the competencies layer, most interventions rely on a few key propensities that can be leveraged, which I have listed above. Using this basic knowledge, a careful observation and interview of stakeholders will usually provide enough information for installation design. The second part of the book shows how to find the relevant propensities in the field.

Interestingly, as seen above, antagonistic motives coexist in the same individual. Living organisms have many such antagonistic systems, which allow them to adjust the behaviour finely and dynamically at the best point of compromise between the two opposing directions. For example, the biceps and triceps muscles are antagonists: one bends the arm, the other stretches it. The hormone glucagon raises blood sugar levels, while insulin lowers them. The same is true of many emotional and cognitive mechanisms: we can love and we can hate; we can be selfish and we can be altruistic. Human beings are excellent learners, curious, creative explorers and manipulators. But they are also cautious and tend to follow the group – because the foolhardy and the loners did not survive.

Evolution is driven by effectiveness, and it preserves those behaviours or organs that contribute to that effectiveness in a serendipitous and opportunistic way. This is why innate propensities or heuristics tend to appear as a mixed bag. This is also why we can harbour contradictory drives: because some can be useful in one situation or another; they can also function as a safeguard against an excess of the opposite drive. For example, we may be easily influenced, but in other circumstances we may show reactance, that is, resistance, and even opposition, to influence.

The existence of antagonist couples of motives is a blessing for the changemaker. Depending how we want to frame a situation, one or another of these propensities will be primed at the forefront of the actor's orientation system. Elicit fear and that will usually inhibit action; elicit curiosity and you may trigger exploration; and so on. Let us always remember that, as a changemaker, we can leverage one or the other of these antagonist motives and mechanisms. We cannot suppress the motives, but we can play on these antagonisms and, for example, leverage sociability to overcome egoist basic needs, and so on.

In sum: embodied competencies are the components of the installation that reside within the person. People bring with them in the installation the propensities for action and a series of mental and physical instruments to perform it. This is how the human competencies are an essential part of the installation and make it work. The installation could not work without its human parts, it would then only be a setting. Just as a restaurant without the personnel and the clients is not a functional restaurant, it is just a building with a kitchen and a big dining room.

We can train the users away from the installations (e.g. at school), but usually users embody the competencies through practice within the installation: they learn by doing or helped by other humans. Installations should be designed with this in mind; therefore they should facilitate first use for novices and learning for all users. There is a nice array of propensities the changemaker can exploit to drive behaviour. The existence of antagonistic tendencies in every human being provides ample opportunity to adjust channelling.

8

The social layer:
regulation by others and society

We have so far considered how an isolated subject behaves in a given situation. But we are never alone; we live in society. Our actions have impact on others, and we are aware of this; conversely others have impact on what we do. Others help us, they can also prevent us from doing something, try to influence us in one way or another. This must be considered, in order to understand why people do what they do and, of course, it can be leveraged to channel people into acting in a desired way, or to prevent them from doing something.

The Lewin experiments

In 1943, in a now classic experiment, Kurt Lewin, the great social psychologist and founder of action research, tried to make Americans eat more offal – at that time of war the government was eager to make better use of food resources. In one group (A) of housewives (the typical family food gatekeeper then), they tried persuasion with nutrition arguments. In another (B), they brought, through discussion, members of the group to decide together and commit to cook offal for their families. So, in group A, information and persuasion. In group B, information and group decision. The results[1] were clear – and confirmed by many similar experiments later: in group A, few (3%) cooked offal. In group B, many more (32%) did. This shows two things: (1) information alone is rarely enough to change behaviour; (2) participation and social commitment can change behaviour. Because humans are social creatures, a person always acts, explicitly or implicitly, as a member of some group. It matters to know what the reference group is to understand their behaviour, predict it and influence it, since the opinion of this group matters to the person.

The general driving force of social regulation is that people usually want to fit in with their community. To do this they will try to behave in a way that they believe is expected by the group to which they want to belong, or at least is accepted by that group. Most mechanisms of social regulation rely on this sociability motive on the part of the subjects and/or those enforcing the regulation. Because humans have evolved as social animals, these mechanisms of social regulation are extremely powerful. Many experiments in social psychology have shown that these social mechanisms can override not only logic and reason, but even override other individual mental and emotional processes. For example, being in a group that (pretends to) perceive something may actually make one perceive that same thing, or at least declare to do so.[2]

History has shown that normal people can do horrible things in groups, things they would never have considered doing individually. They can also do amazing things as a group that they would never have considered individually either. Actually, it is easier to make people change as a group than change individually, because a main reason why people are reluctant to change is that they do not want to differ from the rest of their group. That is precisely what Lewin leveraged.

Content and process of social regulation

Social regulation has two aspects, content and process. Content traces the boundaries of what behaviour is acceptable and expected (e.g. what is considered acceptable as courtship and what is defined as sexual harassment; or, as in the example of Lewin, what is acceptable as food). Process is the means of controlling that actual behaviours indeed stay within these boundaries (e.g. interventions of bystanders, police, family, peers).

The content can be defined more or less precisely, as can the degree of acceptability of the transgression: there are a thousand shades in tracing the line separating the expected from the unacceptable, from formal 'bright line' rules in law to 'fashion' in the way one dresses on that particular beach. The process can use a vast array of different means and devices, which I will describe below. An 'institution' refers to a system that controls content (the set of expected behaviours) and process (the means); so institutions are extremely diverse.

Content (the set of behaviours expected in a given situation by the community) varies across cultures, in time and space, because they are the product of collective decision and practice. In France you may drink wine in public; in some countries you may not. These rules are not always clear and different actors might have different views of interpretations. In addition to the content, the perceptions people have of that content ('social norms') matter; so there are many shades of 'how we do around here' is understood. But the social means of scaffolding and control (the process) are similar across cultures. I will focus here on process.

The same rule (i.e. rights of access to a particular area) can be implemented using different techniques. You can restrict access to an area by installing walls and locks, or guards, or simply a sign forbidding entry. Incidentally, we note that the three layers of an installation can substitute and/or overlap:

channelling can take place through affordances (a wall that prevents access to my property) or embodied competencies (people know not to cross a private fence, even if it is low and symbolic) and/or a 'do not trespass' sign or a guard. Different techniques are associated with different forms of implementation, acceptance, effectiveness and cost. The *content* of social regulation sets boundaries of acceptable/unacceptable behaviour in each situation (in this case 'do not trespass'); boundaries that are socially determined. The *process* of regulation ensures that these boundaries are respected. This is why institutions are both a set of rules and their means of enforcement.

So, the process of social regulation happens through many mechanisms. They can vary from mild incitation to inescapable enforcement. It can be directly performed by humans, as when a mother summons her child to go to bed. It can also operate through media, as with road signs or when the bell rings to announce playtime. At some point, regulation can become embedded in artefacts, such as the motorway toll, or embodied in humans themselves, such as rules for politeness.

Means of social regulation

Among the many means of social regulation, some will be better adapted to the case at hand. Preventing people from stealing nuclear fuel is more critical than preventing them from walking on the lawn of a public park. This has consequences on the tightness with which the regulation must be enforced, and hence on the means by which the regulation should be implemented.

Again, I will not discuss here the content of the rules, only the social means of regulation. Bear in mind that, for most of the means listed, the more people apply the social regulation pressure, and the more consistently they apply it, the greater the effect. Social regulation can operate in two directions:

fostering certain behaviours (obliging people to pay a fare for travelling by train) and preventing some other behaviours (forbidding people to drive on the wrong side of the road). Some means of regulation come from exploiting the propensity of the subjects to spontaneously conform (e.g. imitation, conformism). Some means come at the initiative of others (e.g. vigilante effect, force and threat). In practice most combine both aspects, such as education, which is usually both given and received.

I list these social means of social regulation in no particular order. Most are well known by social psychologists. But strangely these means are underused in most current interventions, because the changemakers tend to think only of what they can do themselves, and they neglect the powerful leverage they can get from people channelling one another in society. So, when designing interventions, come back to this laundry list to check if there is something you could use in your particular case. Managing to leverage a population as one of your means of intervention can produce massive effects at large scale, as shown by some examples described below (see the examples of traffic rules enforcement, and fighting domestic violence).

Imitation and public demonstration

If I attend a ceremony where everyone suddenly stands up, I will do the same. Imitation is the act of replicating the behaviour of others, consciously or unconsciously. People have an innate tendency to imitate others, especially leaders and peers within their group. This is why the testimonials of prominent peers, and the example of leaders are so influential.

Behaviour itself is a medium for the inscription of norms and their display. Exposure to the behaviour of others is a process by which the set of recommended behaviours in the local culture propagates from one person to another through example and imitation. If you succeed in inscribing the desired behaviour on the body of some influential people, they become a walking example for the edification of the masses. The behaviour of other people is a display of the norm, just as the text of a law displays the rule for the benefit of loyal citizens.

At the moment of experience, the inscription in memory connotes the embodiment with a 'value' (good/bad, pleasant/unpleasant, . . .) that is the product of the emotional and cognitive 'effect' of the experience on the watcher. If I see someone horribly punished for some behaviour, I will most likely avoid it myself. Social punishment of perpetrators shows the limits, the degrees of gravity and the effect of forbidden behaviours. When punishment (and its rationale with values) is made public, its effects are more powerful. This effect was used in public executions with torture, which were designed, in dark ages, as a show. Conversely if I see someone publicly rewarded (e.g. with power or recognition), I will be inclined to imitate their behaviour. Society does this with all kinds of installations where good behaviour is recognized, showed and honoured, from cinema awards to medal ceremonies. The degree to which a rule is or is not enforced is also important: if it is known that littering is forbidden, but people think that everyone does it without consequence, many are likely to do it. If some degree of visible enforcement is introduced (by authorities or peers, as discussed below), this could deter a significant proportion of people from engaging in the practice.

In your interventions, think of how you can make good practice visible, and visibly rewarded.

Influence and persuasion

I have already mentioned influence and persuasion: they are socio-cognitive processes by which others can induce us to adopt a given behaviour. Because humans are smart, to produce social regulation they often leverage cognitive mechanisms, as we saw in the previous chapter.

The social nature of the source (who is giving the information) is paramount for its effect. Legitimate and trusted sources, such as from famous people, have stronger effect. The nature of persuasion is to show directly the relationship between cause and effect in such a way that people believe the causal relationship is true. In our case, the means is to show how a certain behaviour (or its absence) can produce a certain result. Another example is the display of memorials to the people who have died, placed on the side of the road where accidents happen (e.g. funeral crosses, wreaths of sympathy).

Societies use persuasion in educational campaigns, but a limitation of these is that persuasion takes place away from the point of action. Explaining why one should adopt a certain behaviour should be done at the moment of orientation, i.e. at the point of action. Let us take an example: During the first Covid-19 pandemic, people were advised to wash their hands to avoid catching and spreading germs. But most people did not know how to wash their hands properly (and neglected some important parts, just quickly rubbing their palms with some soap). Explicit cartoons showing the step-by-step procedure, posted above the sinks in public bathrooms and toilets, at the point of action, persuaded people by showing the how and why of hand washing. The understanding that hands pick up and carry germs was reinforced by the clever use, in some Asian hospitals, of stickers depicting giant Covid-19 viruses, which were placed on doorknobs and other strategic locations, signalling the risk of catching viruses on one's hands.

While most uses of persuasion involve exposing targets to discourse from credible sources, remember that you can be more creative in your interventions. Again, persuasion is about making people believe in the link between a behaviour and a consequence.

Influence, as I explained earlier, is driven by the need to appear consistent. To avoid being confronted with contradictions and the need to justify them, we simply follow the flow of the process, whatever the content of the decision. Therefore, using influence means: suggesting to the subject that he follow a certain path and avoiding exposing him to the possibility of behaving differently. Putting the subject in a situation where behaving differently from what is presented as 'the way things are done around here' would require expressing opposition, justification, or rejection of the rules of sociability, where behaving differently would be socially costly, is the way to go. Typically, placing the target in a group of peers, or even better, people of high status who seem to expect the target behaviour, will expose the target to the social forces of influence. The job of 'influencers' includes making their audience believe that this specific thing to do or to have, which they promote, is the right choice 'because' other (important, trendy, smart, similar to you) people also believe this is the right choice. Note this 'because' is not a rational explanation, it is a social approval. Making social expectations salient and showing others how to conform will put the target in a position to be influenced.

There are many ways in which social influence operates. Nevertheless, they mostly exploit two embodied propensities: (1) people prefer to be consistent with the other members of their group; (2) they prefer to be consistent with themselves and avoid dissonance. However, because individuals like to have freedom and control over what they do, they tend to reject what they perceive as an attempt to influence them ('reactance'). Therefore, attempts to persuade or influence should be light-handed to avoid reactance. Parents who try to teach their children a behaviour (e.g. making their bed) have observed that, when the children see their peers doing it, they adopt spontaneously the very same behaviour they rejected when their parents repeatedly told them to do it. Since reactance is more a rejection of the process of being socially pressured than a rejection of the content of the demand itself, it may happen that the rejection of the behaviour happens with the parents, but not elsewhere; e.g. children will not make their bed at home but will do it when spending a night at friends.

Influence can also exploit the desire to belong to the group, when the target behaviour appears as a condition to be a good member of the group. Influence dovetails well with making good practice visible, as described earlier with imitation, and with assigning roles and status (see below). These three means of action go well together in implementation.

Role, status and the social contract

Role and status are involved in social regulation by providing learned expectations of how people should behave in a given situation.[3] Your role is the set of behaviours that people legitimately expect from you, given your social position. Your status is the set of behaviours you can legitimately expect from people, given your social position.[4] For example, if you are a parent, in this role you are expected to educate and care for your children; and in this status you can expect your children to obey you, at least in response to reasonable requests. A role is part of a social contract that the person has accepted as a condition of enjoying their status. Once a person has accepted their role, they will tend to stick to it,[5] sometimes at the expense of their own interest.

Role and status are the individualized versions of the social contract that determines our group belonging and position in society, our social self. A social contract is what links the status to the role: 'If you do this, you get that.' The social contract combines the necessity of predictability that enables society to exist and the personal interests of the individual. Social contracts are at the root of organization and the division of labour. In a way, they come to define what a person thinks she is, just as group affiliation does. Therefore, people will feel engaged and committed to their role and status.

In society, what is done, and what is revealed,[6] must match the social contract. Otherwise, there is a breach and people lose face,[7] not to mention the possibility of litigation; such breaches call for 'repair'. When addressing someone by their role, you summon them to act accordingly, in the name of society.

Role and status are essential to humans in society, and hence they are extremely powerful determinants of behaviour. In fact, they can be stronger than influence, authority, and even some basic instincts (e.g. fear, sexual drive). Many psychological experiments have shown the strength of the social contract; in some cases, people are led to behave in ways that appear weird, such as in the famous Milgram experiment,[8] in which subjects, accepting the role of an experimenter, inflict on people strong electric shocks in the framework of a 'learning experiment'.

The social contracts regulate interactions: they specify what respective behaviours are expected. A society is a set of people who consent to the same set of social contracts, i.e. to behave according to their given role, and according to other people's status in their interaction with them. This requires that each person has competencies as a 'generalized other' – that is, someone who knows the contracts and can behave not only in their own role in the different situations they may encounter but also as 'the other' when they meet people who are playing their own role. For example, as a customer you know how to behave as the 'other' to the salesperson who approaches you in a shop; or how to respond as the 'friendly local' to the stranger who asks you for directions in your own street. In other words, we are all like comedians who know the play, and know not only our own roles, but also those of others. A good society is a system where the transactions are regulated by social contracts in such a way that transactions are satisficing for the parties, and that there are no catastrophic emergent effects from the global set of transactions.

This has several implications for interventions. First a caveat: changing the nature of very usual social contracts – for example, regarding gender, hierarchical relations, or parent/ child interactions – has impact on the set of competencies of the generalized other, the basic set of competencies of *every* loyal member of the society. That is why such societal changes take time to adjust, because they need the consent and cooperation of everyone.

Note that changes in the usual social contracts often trigger debates about values. Indeed, the provision of value is the expected outcome of interactions. What has value is what contributes to satisfying a motive; value is always a latent variable in behaviour. So social contracts, which regulate how one satisfies motives, are connected to values. Think of the examples above about relations at work or in the family: changing the social contracts will impact the power balance, the expectations and the satisfaction of participants, by modifying the rules of conduct.

Second, in the installation itself, roles and statuses of the employees of the installation, as well as roles and statuses of its users, are part of its design. The clearer that roles and statuses are spelled out and displayed, the better. And it matters to consider how the definition of roles and statuses enables the various stakeholders to fulfil their motives (which we will see in the implementation chapters).

Conformity and zeal

Conformity refers to the phenomenon of individuals following the norm and doing what they think others do or expect them to do. Because it's based on people's perceptions rather than reality, you don't necessarily have to change what everyone else is doing to influence others, just their perceptions of what others are doing. The motive may be to avoid standing out and being identified as different, but it may also be for the sheer pleasure of feeling involved and part of the group. Some crowd behaviours (marching, cheering) are examples of this warm feeling of participation.

Zeal refers to individuals who go beyond mere conformity and voluntarily engage in 'exemplary' compliance, with the motive to get recognition and position in the group. In most groups there will be people who are in search of affiliation and status; these people will be most prone to conformity and zealotry. Think of political or religious extremists, who want to prove they belong by appearing more radical. While these compliant subjects and zealots may seem like a bargain to the changemaker, it should always be remembered that their main motive is rarely the goal of the behaviour itself, but to be recognized as a member of the group and to please the group. This means that the real lever of their channelling is the group opinion – so do not be surprised if they change their tune; and you will know how to act if you want them to change.

Instruction and guidance

Education, instruction and training given by other people and organizations help individuals learn social skills and ways to understand things. These skills help people interact with others and follow rules. When people are unsure of what to do, they look to others for information, they are open to their influence and listen. As hinted above regarding role and status, training the personnel of an installation and its users is necessary. This training process is also part of the installation design, especially if the roles require competencies that are non-standard. Display of the rules at the entry of the installation is a usual feature (e.g. 'no smoking', speed limit).

Vigilante effect

This refers to the phenomenon whereby individuals act as representatives of the 'Generalized Other' to remind and enforce norms. Every loyal member of a community is a watchdog for others: this is the 'vigilante effect'. For example, as I was cycling home from work, I passed a woman who was cycling with her phone in her hand, video-conferencing and showing the city to her contact. As I passed this reckless cyclist, I told her, 'What you are doing is crazy, it is very dangerous.'

Each person constantly reminds others of how to behave on behalf of society, by encouraging or reprimanding postures, facial expressions, speech and actions. Staff of the installation are expected to play this vigilante role in a formal way. In many installations, especially large ones, other users will usually play the vigilante role spontaneously, e.g. to get others to stay in line, to keep quiet in libraries.

There are different shades of getting someone back on track. At one end of the spectrum is the Good Samaritan, who guides a foreigner through the process of buying a train ticket. At the other, the person who reports to the police a neighbour who has littered the street. Usually, a frown or a look is the minimal means by which the vigilante reminds his fellow citizen of 'the way we do things around here'. This is sufficient, because the vigilante acts as a representative of the Generalized Other, and her corralling action reminds the target that everyone 'around here' is supposed to act according to 'the way we do things around here'. Since, as we have seen, humans are social animals and very sensitive to the expectations of other members of their community, a gentle reminder is usually sufficient.

The vigilante effect will occur naturally once you have managed to make the target behaviour the new normal. This is the benefit of success. However, it can be armed and encouraged. One way is to encourage denunciation (not recommended in most instances as it can easily backfire or encumber regulating authorities). Another is to facilitate direct intervention by creating gentle ways to bring misbehavers back on track. This is done by channelling the action of potential bystanders, who might otherwise feel afraid or unsure to intervene in a relatively low-conflict and 'acceptable' way. In Mayor Mockus' famous traffic-enforcement intervention in Bogotá, 400 mime artists acted as silent vigilantes, gently taunting drivers who ignored red lights, and jaywalkers. Then, once the objective was clear, thumbs-up/thumbs-down cards distributed to the population to express their approval or disapproval of their fellow citizens' behaviour resulted in 350,000 equipped vigilantes in Bogotá. This distributed social control accounts for an effect size (halving the number of road casualties!) that would be beyond the reach of traditional public policies. In that case, the secret was boosting 'mutual regulation' by citizens, at a cost and on a scale that would be impossible to achieve through more traditional means of regulation (as you can't have a policeman or build a barrier in each corner . . .).

Force, threat and reward

Communities usually have dedicated police forces entitled to correct, by physical constraint or punishment, those who do not comply with the rules. The mere existence of these special bodies for control and enforcement is usually sufficient to threaten and prevent rule-breaking behaviour. While these mechanisms may appear coercive or punitive, they in fact work both ways, and may reward those who behave well through gaining access, kudos and reputation. Playing one's role properly provides the benefit of the status that goes with the role. Many installations formalize and gamify this reward process by giving good users recognition and privileges (e.g. gold member, loyalty card, reward points, social credit). These techniques can be used in the design of installations to leverage social regulation.

Some readers may be surprised not to see laws appearing in this list. That is because a law is about the *content* of the regulation; the *means* by which a law is implemented in installations are many and include some listed above, especially force and threat (police, justice), and instruction ('ignorance of the law is no excuse'). What distinguishes the law from other types of content, such as norms or good practice, is its formal and official character, and a stronger weight, which makes compliance compulsory and violations punishable. In this way, the law brings a stronger social bright line, even though in principle it is one more set of required or forbidden behaviours in 'the way we do things here'. Note also that the ways in which law is changed are different from other practices, and their geographical scope is often beyond the immediate reach of the changemaker. They involve a different set of actors and intervention techniques, requiring specific allies and agencies.

In summary, there are many shades in 'the set of expected behaviours'; the content of social regulation varies from recommended custom (the way people eat their soup) to bright line rules that are extremely explicit (do not kill) and enforced with severe punishment. In between are hundreds of shades, including norms, regulation by technology, jurisprudence, rules of trade, good practice, etc.

To address in society the now-what? question, because we need cooperation, we must assume we are all on the same page, that we play in the same game, that we refer to a common reality, which we construct and change together. We need to act with common frames of reference, and to act according to the same social contacts of 'that is the way we do things here'. And we need to be assured that others do indeed share the same frame of references – e.g. that on the road the driver coming the other way will indeed stay on his side of the road. This assumes that we have the same interpretation of the situation ('what you see is what I see') and therefore that we can refer to the same set of reciprocal expectations of behaviour.

This implicit 'what you see is what I see', is a *psychosocial pact* that founds the possibility of life in common, which is not a trivial hypothesis considering that we all see the world differently, according to our position and experience.

Nevertheless, it should be remembered that (especially in less 'organized' societies) while there are many people who share the same psychosocial pact, expectations and social contracts, there is often a percentage (which may not be negligible) of people who do not, because they are unaware or because they choose to resist (see the example of jaywalking). Dealing with these specific populations may be a simple question of education, but it may also be a question of ideological divergence, which should then be addressed politically.

The content of social regulation is implemented through a variety of mechanisms that work together to enforce correct behaviour as defined by institutions. These means include imitation, influence, persuasion, role and status expectations in the social contract, conformity and zeal, instruction and guidance, vigilante effect, force threat and reward. These means can overlap, and all tend to the same. This regulation layer operates for empowering; it also works well for control.

Social forces are a powerful tool. Consider school education, where teacher and peer influence are paramount. Another case is brainwashing, which efficiently leverages these social forces to 'convert' war prisoners (and populations) to a new way of 'this is how we see things here'. But in general, in deliberate and systematic behavioural change interventions, social forces, apart from social norms, tend to be under-used.

I advise to always consider using these powerful forces, and to check the list of means above but to proceed with caution, as with any powerful medicine. They can backfire or have some serious side effects by raising the instincts of imitation and aggression. Be mindful of which values you put forward when calling for social regulation, and foster encouragement rather than enforcement.

9

The combination of layers: redundancy, resilience and evolution

We examined successively three types of channelling components in the layers of affordances, embodied competencies and social regulation, and how they can be implemented in installations. Good installations combine components from several different layers to efficiently channel behaviour at each step of activity. These layers are not independent of one another, and their combination produces powerful effects.

Redundancy and resilience

A most useful effect of the multilayered aspect of installations is their resilience, which results from the redundancy of their components in channelling action. If one layer fails to channel the behaviour, the others will. For example, in the car my passenger forgets to put on her seat belt; as I try to start the car, a warning signal beeps. Here, the embodied competencies of my passenger failed, but the affordances layer of the installation stepped in to channel the behaviour. It could also have been the social layer of the installation: I could myself have reminded my passenger to buckle up. Or perhaps both: as the warning rings, I may tell the passenger to please buckle up.

Human embodied competence is often called upon to fix issues in the affordance layer. At the supermarket, when the barcode reader fails to read the code on a product, the human cashier steps in, reads the code and enters it into the machine. Often, two layers will combine to fix the faulty installation: I am blocked at the door of the building because I do not know the access code. I call upon someone who knows the code, and that person gives it to me. Here I used both my embodied competencies (knowing how to call someone) and the social regulation of that other person who checks whether I am allowed to enter. Two things happened here. First, resilience: the installation is resilient enough to channel behaviour, even when people are incompetent (e.g. novice, oblivious), or when the material equipment is faulty, or when there is no clear and explicit rule. So, the installation is capable, with its resilient multilayered structure, of producing correct behaviour on the spot at the point of action, *now*.

Furthermore, and that is the second aspect, reconstruction, the installation is also capable of fixing or reconstructing itself for future operation. In the door code example above, once I have embodied the code, next time I will be able to open the door by myself. I have learned in doing: my competencies have been fixed. Not only does the resilience of the installation enable me to perform correctly the first time and attain my goal (door open), but it has also the power of constructing a full, and even more resilient installation by making a fix that is more than a repair, a construction. Even more amazing is that I will now myself become part of this increased resilience: if another person gets stuck at the door, I can give that person the code! Every learner becomes a potential teacher for others (and a potential vigilante).

Through installations, structure constructs practice, and practice reconstructs structure, as per Anthony Giddens' structuration theory.[1] Installations are the building cells of that societal process that enables societies to operate, grow, sustain and evolve. A society comprises the many components of its installations, the social contracts that bind its members, and the values that underlie these contracts.

Natural evolution of the system

As we see, installations are powerful devices. They are naturally adapted to humans, precisely as they leverage the natural assets of humans: tools, knowledge, society. That is not by chance: it is humans who have invented installations to empower and control themselves and others with minimal effort; so they naturally leveraged their usual devices: tools, their mind and other people. In fact, humans co-evolved with their installations. Just as bees co-evolved with their beehives, humans co-evolved with the gigantic human-hives we know as civilizations; and this co-evolution continues.

Every installation is in continuous reconstruction by its users and, in that process, some components change and impact the other components. The various layers of an installation do not remain static. They reconstruct and evolve through practice, replacement, accidental change, and deliberate innovation. We could for example consider how old canteens evolved into modern self-service cafeterias, adopting the model of the assembly line rather than of the banquet. But perhaps the reader has had enough of cafeterias, so let us illustrate with the example of school classes. School classes have existed for centuries, but today's classes differ from those in the Middle Ages, from those a hundred years ago and even from those twenty years ago. This, even though the purpose (education) remained the same. It is interesting to see how these changes happened. They concern the three layers: digital tools have replaced the pen and exercise book (and chalk and slate before); the competencies of the pupils have changed (today they type better than they handwrite); the rules have changed (teachers do not hit pupils with rulers, pupils are encouraged to participate, etc.).

Because installations are made of several layers, the evolution of the layers can happen to some extent independently, even though the evolution of one layer must always remain compatible with the rest of the installation. Each layer is regenerated at its own rhythm, as components age, decay, or when they are replaced by better ones that become available. In the class, pupils change every year, teachers change at a slower rhythm, some equipment stays for a long time (tables, chairs) and others are replaced frequently (books), programmes and regulations tend to change with national or local governance. A change in one of the components may induce a change in another component: e.g. the introduction of chemistry classes impacted the nature of the teaching rooms and equipment, which in turn opened new formats for tutorials that could be applied to other disciplines, and so on. In use, there is a drive for betterment of satisfaction by improvement of the installation, which provokes gradual changes, drifts, and innovation. Practice reconstructs structure, but a structure that is not exactly identical.

As a result, the installation will (unless it fails and disappears) usually get better and fix itself as it gets used, each layer improving under the pressure of the two others. Imports from other installations happen. For example, classroom blackboards were gradually replaced by whiteboards, then by digital display, with devices that were imported from the meeting rooms of industry. New practices and skills are imported in a given installation carried by the human users themselves, who acquired them in other installations. For example, students brought into schools digital literacy learned at home with their own devices.

Installation theory is about the way societies change, piecemeal and locally. Now that we understand the natural process, we can intervene, deliberately, to orient the change. That is the purpose of the second part of the book.

Part 2

How to change behaviour

10

The behaviour change
intervention process step by step

Our purpose is to create a new behavioural path for a given activity. For example, to satisfy the same motive (e.g. transport, thermal comfort, nutrition) with less impact on the environment, or better health. To this effect we will design installations that channel the behaviour all along this new desired path.

What matters is to take the perspective of the subjects in the situation, and provide them with a behavioural path that is easy to identify, which appears to satisfice their motives and be safe; a path where all the tools are available with obvious affordances, where action does not require complex information search or mental effort, where action is consistent with their beliefs, and where acting so confirms or reinforces their belonging to their social group.

The general idea is to make sure that proper components of an installation are implemented at the point of action to channel users in the desired direction. We want to signpost, scaffold and control the trajectory *at each step* of activity. And, where needed, we will consider changing or adding components. Exploring in systematic manner, at each step, the three layers (affordances, competencies, regulation) facilitates finding creative ideas.

Every combination of activity and context is different; therefore designing installations is more art than science. We will have to make trade-offs between what we would like to do and what we can actually do, between vision and agency. I will address the various issues one by one, starting with a general overview of the design process and the requirements for a sustainable installation. Then we will get into the detail of implementation.

The process is as follows. First, we analyse the current situation: by observing the activity and discussing with users and other stakeholders, we understand the motivations and goals of the parties involved. We identify the pain points and the relevant stakeholders. We list what we find in an 'activity grid'. Then we decide where to intervene. Taking into account our agency, we look at which levels of the installation it is most efficient and cost-effective to set up channelling devices. In doing so, we make sure that the different stakeholders are rewarded in a balanced way for their contribution, that there is a fair social contract and that the underlying business model is sustainable.

We test feasibility at an experimental scale and assess impact. We then modify the intervention before full implementation and scale-up. This approach is similar to classic design thinking, but it differs in several ways. First, it always starts from the activity (not from the product, people or business). The key question is: What are people trying to do here? Why? What are the motives? What are the goals?

For the changemaker, the initial call for intervention may be about a product, a business, a problem, an installation. But this is not the best way of framing the issue. You should first take a step back and understand what the activity is. Because the solid compass for design is the motive; it is the motive that drives the action. You have to find the motive – or find them, because there may be several. Starting from the activity ensures that the user is at the centre of the process.

For example, suppose I want to save water when I take showers. The main motive of the activity is to get washed; saving water is a secondary motive. If what I propose to do to save water interferes too much with getting washed, the solution will not work. Another example: Suppose I want to reduce pollution in the city and promote public transport to improve health and protect the environment. My solutions should not get in the way of the motives behind the activity of private transport, which includes transport, of course, but may also include other motives like flexibility, autonomy, safety and privacy in getting around. The new trade-offs of my solution should at least minimally satisfice these other motives or offer a worthwhile compensation.

The second difference is that our approach examines the activity in a systematic and structured way, considering each of the three layers step by step (not just product design, user experience or rules alone); hence it is called multilayered. We start from an analysis of the problem, never from a solution (to keep an open mind), and we systematically explore the three dimensions of determinant components at each step. For example, if we want to study a problem related to food, we will follow the users in their whole food activity, starting from the phase when they decide to get food, then to the shop, how they buy, transport, store, cook, eat and finally dispose of the waste. At each step, we will record in detail the relevant components (e.g. availability in shops, cooking competencies, kitchen equipment, consumer tastes) and discuss them with the users. We will also interview other stakeholders we meet along the way (dietitians, retailers, restaurants, etc.). It is not difficult, but it is a lot of work.

Finally, our approach takes seriously the involvement of the participants ('do with, rather than do for', as I will detail below): it considers them as genuine design partners and future components of the installation, enrolled in the process of improving the activity, rather than considering them as targets of behavioural change. Of course, all design approaches claim to involve users; but, often, that is done superficially, with some surveys and possibly a consultation. We rather go into the field, in depth.

I must admit the superficial approach has attractions. Frankly, it is a pain to seriously involve the users. It is costly, and takes time and effort. It makes it almost impossible to describe the final result from the start because you do not know what users will come up with. You will have to let go, and accept that while you are in control of the process, you are not in control of the content. That makes it difficult to plan costs and timing, and can become a serious problem with sponsors, who are understandably reluctant to give a blank cheque. Discussions with users also may raise early resistance and cause unpredictable delays. You are warned.

Nevertheless, I maintain that serious user involvement is worthwhile in the long run. All the issues you avoid or ignore by superficially involving users at the design stage are likely to come back to bite you at the implementation and scale-up stage, at many times the cost. The reason why superficial practices continue is, unfortunately, that the designers, and sometimes their sponsors, are usually gone by the time problems arise. So they can get away with it. This kind of behaviour has been described, in the candid language of a major industry where I worked, as 'running faster than the shit you spread'. Please do not do that, it is unprofessional.

The spirit of intervention: a local approach

As said above, the phase of analysis and discussion with stakeholders is necessary and useful. Some stakeholders will feel they lose in the change, and that feeds resistance. An honest attempt to reach a compromise that is acceptable to most parties, and that compensates them for loss, is a way forward.

With such a process, the outcome will also be more stable and benefit from the contribution of all, or at least from minimal opposition. This requires communication, consultation, and subsidiarity (doing at a higher level only what cannot be done at a more local level). This collaborative approach is especially important for interventions involving large organizations and policy makers,[1] to get their support and buy-in. Failing to do this is likely to arouse their suspicion, elicit resistance and possibly generate a strong reaction.

At local level, this analysis and discussion phase turns out to be a practical design process rather than a discussion of high-level principles. Concrete discussion of the activity allows clarification of which behaviour is acceptable and should be channelled. In such discussions, it is usually easier to discuss practical, local implementation because specific *local* solutions can be found – e.g. for vegetarianism, which menus to present, and when.

It is a general observation that local solutions are easier to find than generic solutions, simply because resources and constraints vary, and what is possible in one place may not be possible in another. Said differently: often problems that have no generic solution may still have many local solutions. Not all local problems require a global solution. Think about transport: the local terrains call for different solutions; the city is not like the countryside

A generic issue can also be divided into several more local or smaller issues, which can be addressed with different approaches and installations. In different branches or steps of an activity, the point of action is different; this means discussion with different stakeholders, different affordances, also different local rules. For example, we can design interventions to channel people into fewer unwanted pregnancies – and better implement the socially agreed solutions for those that still occur; we can minimize the occurrence of painful end of life with prevention – and better implement the socially

agreed solutions for such moments; we can prevent dangerous behaviour – and better address those that still occur. But,
depending on the target, the culture, the type of situation (e.g.
the stage of child conception), solutions will differ.

These negotiations with stakeholders are more likely to succeed if they are local and specific, because it is easier to find a
local solution than a generic one that would gracefully apply
to all specific cases that differ by population, climate, culture,
history, economy, etc. And, indeed, local solutions are different; what works here and now may not work there and then.
Think of agriculture, housing or clothing. Or, for the same
problem, the aspect of stock vs flow (for health care, pollution,
poverty, . . .): taking care of the current stock (of patients, CO_2,
victims, . . .) is one aspect, and stopping the incoming flow is
another.

Although this may seem a paradox, the local approach
(in an organization, a city, a region) opens a realistic way
of addressing the *global* problems of societal transition on
a large scale. Scaling up can be done by multiplying locally
adapted interventions, rather than applying top-down,
generic, one-size-fits-all policies. For example, if we want to
save resources like water and energy, this can only be done
by multiplying local savings in very diverse situations. A local
approach involves local negotiation; at that scale it can be
done with stakeholder participation, empowerment, subsidiarity, diffusion by example. Such processes are compatible
with autonomy, individual initiative, human relations and
democracy; which often come with better well-being. They
are also compatible with small-scale, flexible funding and
resource provision systems.

The changemaker should be aware that discussions on
generic principles can easily become polarized, and prone to
involve non-local stakeholders, whose own agenda may com-
plicate the process without positive impact. For example, the
press is mostly interested in catching attention, activists in

promoting their ideology, political parties in national elections. So, it is good to hear a variety of stakeholders, but to stay focused on the local installation in discussion. Nevertheless, it is often necessary to take into account some generic constraints (typically, laws – but in a later step these can be changed).

If stakeholders are reluctant to implement a particular type of intervention, then another type needs to be found. On the other hand, if they are happy with a radical type of intervention, so be it. Experience shows that regulation is a powerful tool that can solve many thorny problems arising from the selfish and horizon-bound aspects of human behaviour. Regulation should always be considered among the potential solutions. People tend to overestimate the resistance to regulation; usually, after some initial lobbying by those who believe they will be negatively affected, once the regulation is in place people (and corporations too) adapt quite quickly, comply and even wonder why things were different in the past.

Finally, because activity is an embodied process, nothing can replace first-hand human experience in assessing its quality. It would be foolish to plan interventions without seriously involving users in the design process, from beginning (demand) to end (evaluation). This is necessary to truly understand the perceptions, feelings and emotions at stake. Ideally, everyone involved in the intervention, including the changemaker, should have experienced the activity they want to channel, if only to truly understand what users are saying.

Although the above seems like common sense, it is not usually practised. Sometimes changemakers are bound by ideology, especially if they are responsible for public policies that they believe should conform to their party's political programme. Nudging, for example, is about using psychological mechanisms to influence, but only when they are compatible with libertarian paternalism: that is, offering a preferred choice but never forcing it. Such an approach, which does not consider regulation, can limit the power of intervention.

We tend to attribute causes to individuals rather than to situations, and this attribution bias, shared by scientists, explains the over-emphasis on embodied competencies that is common in behavioural interventions. But making the individual who bears the symptom the cause of problems is also a convenient way of shifting responsibility for change to individuals, avoiding systemic social action that is politically difficult or costly for some influential economic actors.

More often, solid consultation with stakeholders and targets is skipped or botched simply because the changemaker or its sponsors prefer to cut corners. This may seem like a good idea at the time, but they usually pay dearly later when what they have neglected comes back to bite them.

Activity analysis

Activity analysis is the key to good intervention. This is where what was explained in Part 1 comes in handy. You need to draw a detailed timeline of the activity trajectory. Start this with the trajectory of the main type of user (e.g. the consumer), and follow, step by step, what they do. Do not settle for oral descriptions given by users, observe actual practice. As you do, fill in the activity grid (see Figure 5), which lists, step by step, the actions, the motives, the subgoals, the relevant components in the three layers of the installation, the other actors and stakeholders who intervene at the step.

And, of course, add your notes: is this step problematic? Why? Does it bring specific benefits? Which ones? Our objective is to represent behaviour in order to make our decisions about which intervention to take. For this we need some kind of map. The activity grid will be that map, allowing a systematic approach to scouring the activity for potential intervention points. The activity trajectory will serve as a timeline to order

Task	Actor's Motives and Goals	Contributions from Actor	Actor's Rewards	Affordances	Competences	Regulation	Comments
XXX	XXX	XXX	XXX	XXX	XXX	XXX	XXX
Etc. Make as many lines as there are steps	XXX	XXX	XXX	XXX	XXX	XXX	XXX

Figure 5 Typical activity grid structure (see below for concrete examples).

the various steps that are potential intervention points at the natural joints of the activity.

At each step, we need to understand which components of the installation do the channelling. Because the action is distributed, there can be many components. The three layers of the installation are like three main dimensions onto which the components can be projected. A component can be projected onto several layers (e.g. a rule can be social and embodied): it does not matter. What is important is to identify the relevant components and put them on the map – which we do by listing them in the grid. For example, consider 'a one-way street'. This is best coded as a social layer, even though it includes affordance aspects (you can actually drive in it) and embodied aspects (to understand that it is a road).

My colleagues and I make a column for each layer of the installations; we also keep a column for open comments. You can build your own model of activity grid: there are many ways to feed a cat. Just make sure you have written the list of the various steps of the activity of interest, with detailed description of who does what, why, and what the issues are at that point. For example, Figure 6 is the grid of my own home morning routine on workdays. In this routine, there are several steps. After I wake up, I shave, take a shower, prepare breakfast, get dressed, eat breakfast, put dishes in the dishwasher, put on my coat, my bike helmet and leave. This is a simple grid: one actor, linear and straightforward tasks. My main motives here are to go to work fed and dressed, with minimal time and effort. Also, to behave sustainably; but honestly that second motive remains secondary. The purpose of my intervention was to make my routine more sustainable, without losing too much time or comfort.

There were 'pain points' where the routine could be improved. One was that the water is not immediately hot for the shower. Because the electric hot water tank (that heats water during the night, away from peak hours) is located

Task	Actor's Motives and Goals	Contributions from Actor	Actor's Rewards	Affordances	Competences	Regulation	Comments
Wake up	Start new day. Hear the news. Get out of bed.	Get up.	Feel ready on time.	Radio alarm clock.	Setting up alarm.	Working hours.	Alarm clock not easy to programme.
Wash up	Get shaved and clean.	Shave, clean.	Feel clean.	Hot water. Shaving cream. Razor. Shower. Shampoo. Towel.	Shaving and showering.	On weekdays, pressure from family to use the bathroom.	Waste of water while waiting for shower to warm.
Get dressed	Have appearance adapted to the day's activities and weather.	Getting dressed. Possibly check advice with partner.	Feel equipped.	Clean clothes and shoes, adapted to weather and situation.	Knowledge of suitable attire and fitting (shoe lacing, tie knotting etc.)	Dress code.	
Breakfast	Hunger and nutrition.	Prepare and eat breakfast. Clean up.	Enjoying food. Being fed.	Equipped kitchen, kettle, bread, bread, toaster, butter, jam, tea or coffee, table, cutlery.	Preparing tea and toast. Knowledge of partner's preferences.	Diet. Working hours. Transport schedule.	Waiting time in front of toaster and kettle. Tea too hot.
Leaving home	Going to work.	Leave house in order. Take relevant items for the day.	Feel prepared.	Transport. House keys. Charged telephone.	Knowledge of transport time to destination.	Partner's needs. Work or appointment hours and location.	

Figure 6 Activity grid of the author's morning routine before re-installation.

several metres from the bathroom, the first water to flow in the shower is cold 'pipe' water. So, every morning, I used to let the water flow from the shower directly into the drain until it reaches the right temperature. This lasted about 35 seconds and wasted about four litres of pipe water on average. Another pain point: my tea was often too hot to drink it, which made me wait until it cooled at the end of the breakfast, or go to the kitchen to add some cold water to my mug.

I considered several solutions, including relocating the tank closer, but that was too complicated and costly. Finally, my intervention was as follows. Targeting the showering step (line #2 in the grid), (1) I relocated our watering can from the balcony to the shower, to let the pipe-water flow into it until it reaches the right temperature. (2) I changed the order of steps, to turning on, right after getting out of bed, the automatic tea kettle *before* shaving, so it heats while I shave and shower. We have a smart kettle that, when water reaches the chosen temperature, automatically dips the tea into the water for the chosen time, so you only need to start it; it stops by itself. Also now, as I turn on the kettle, I take the butter out of the fridge and put the bread in the toaster – *before* shaving. As a result of changing the order of the steps, once I leave the shower and have dressed, the tea and toast are ready, the toast and tea have started to cool, and the butter is at the right temperature and softer. (3) I slightly reduced the amount of water I pour into the tea kettle. This results in a stronger tea, which I dilute with a small amount of cold tap water before bringing the kettle to the table, with the final effect of having a cooler tea and sparing the energy of heating that extra water to 95°C. That is a marginal energy saving but comes with more comfort and saves time.

I discussed this with my partner and now this has become a routine, saving something around 1,400 litres of water per year. Indeed, now we draw less water from the tap to water the plants, since the watering can is already filled with pipe water. As a bonus, I saved a few minutes of waiting time in front of the toaster and kettle, or filling up the watering can when watering plants. The presence of the watering can next to the shower serves as a savings affordance reminder. I could further improve my routine if I shaved while showering but this is unpractical with our current bathroom setup. Recently my partner put a timer next to the shower, to reduce showering time.

In this simple example, a change of local affordances (watering can location), competencies (reordering steps) and regulation (agreeing on new house rules) improved the activity at no cost, with individual and environmental benefits. This example is not as anecdotal as it seems. The problems with societal challenges such as climate change are the scale of the problem and the locus of control. We will solve these only if everyone, at their local scale, participates. If all households did what we did for the shower, vast amounts of water would be saved. By looking at your own routines, at home, at work, and so on, you will see that there are dozens of activity steps where you could improve and reduce your footprint. Take food. Simply putting a lid on pans reduces energy consumption and heats them up faster (try it!). And, by selecting the products you use, you can help to drive out of business those companies that damage the planet, and encourage the sustainable ones.

Of course, the same can be said of organizations and companies if they review their activities. The agency of humans comes from the number and the distribution of labour. So far, this human agency, let loose, has plundered the planet. The same agency can restore it, but that means (only) a distributed and thoughtful effort of us all. That may not be as difficult as it seems.

Now consider a professional example. Our aim was to redesign a virtual reality (VR) platform to better host virtual conferences (these were the very early days of such platforms). The original platform had glitches. It supported rather well the activity of listening to conference presentations and the avatars looked good, but it did not support well the informal social encounters that are so important in such venues, where people come to learn and disseminate, and also to network with other professionals of the same trade. Analysis here is more complicated, with diverse participants and stakeholders and interweaving tracks, therefore the activity grid has many lines. To make the activity grids simpler, we draw separate grids by type of stakeholder and sub-activity (e.g. onboarding, giving presentation).

To fill in the grids, it is easier to proceed gradually. First, list the main steps of the activities at coarse grain to get an overview. This will be done for each major type of participant. For a conference attendee who also wants to give a presentation, we can distinguish twelve major tasks, from becoming aware of the conference to follow-up once the conference is over (Figure 7). Because the participant will be both a presenter and attendee, there will be steps from the perspective of both presenter and audience.

Each task can be looked at in more detail for possible improvement. For example, based on the feedback given by participants, we knew there was an issue regarding the support of informal networking. This networking usually takes place during breaks and transitions between formal presentations. Compared to conferences in person, where one meets people in the corridors, the cafeteria and social spaces, the virtual platform did not include good installations for informal encounters between avatars and networking.

Interestingly also, while for most participants we observed only Steps 1 to 11, for some participants Step 12, 'troubleshooting technical issues with the helpdesk', took a lot of time and spoiled the experience. This was made worse because, to access the helpdesk, one needed to have a communication channel; alas, the most frequent cause for troubleshooting was that the very access to the conference, the VR channel, was faulty (e.g.

1. **Awareness.** Getting info/invitation: there is a conference at this specific time and place, about such and such topics.
2. **Timetabling.** Planning, booking, solving authorization issues (clearance from organization, funding).
3. **Preparation.** Writing, reviewing, and editing presentation, coordination with organizers and tech support.
4. **Onboarding.** Connecting to and exploration of the digital platform; may include installing and testing the Installation.
5. **Orientation.** Creating more detailed activity plans once more aware of resources on-site.
6. **Presentation giving.** Speaker to audience, data display, moderation, speaker interaction in panels.
7. **Presentation processing.** Taking notes, automatic translation, Interaction with Speaker (Q&A, applause, etc.)
8. **Workshops.** N to N participant interaction, producing collective outputs for proceedings.
9. **Virtual visits and socializing.** Meeting people, informal conversation, exchange of details.
10. **Disembarking.** Changing settings, uninstalling software, rearranging workstations.
11. **Follow-up.** Storage/retrieval of material and contacts from the conference, sharing of material.
12. **Troubleshooting.** Fixing technical and connection issues, especially sound, firewall blocks, and reconnecting.

Figure 7   High-level list of steps in the activity of participating in a conference, for an attendee who also gives a presentation.

firewall issues). This forced participants to use another channel (email, chat, phone, SMS). As a matter of fact, the conference organizers, who were the main contacts for most participants, spent a considerable amount of time answering help requests and solving issues along with the technical helpdesk, instead of playing their role as social facilitator. This impacted one of their activity steps, where they could not contribute as expected: 'creating a networking ambiance' by making introductions and engaging conversations during breaks. Solving technical problems also took time away from participants. Time they would have preferred to have spent networking. Figure 8 shows in

Task	Actor's Motives and Goals	Contributions from Actor	Actor's Rewards	Affordances	Competences	Regulation	Comments
B&T-4 Relational Culture. Create ambience and environment appropriate to networking and social relational goals of the conference.	Encourage social interaction among participants. Deliver high value and memorable relational experiences for presenters and attendees.	**Provide friendly support to participants during onboarding process.** Become familiar with relational goals of presenters. **Approach others and be available to start and engage in conversations.** **Make introductions for presenters and attendees.** **Seed conversations with greetings and introductions.**	Observations and reports of social interaction during transitions and breaks. Expressed satisfaction of presenters and attendees.	Designated spaces for avatar groupings. Availability and receptivity of avatars for interaction. **Support staff availability for navigation and communication prompts.**	Competence for creating a socially magnetic milieu for participants to network with one another. Social 'radar' for noting when mingling is not working 'just right.'	Regulatory norms and VRtiquette promoting openness of new connections yet move participants along to meet others if they freeze up other participants in a manner disallowing a continuous flow of new connections.	*Organizers cannot do properly because they are busy fixing technical issues.*

Figure 8 Social facilitation of breaks and transitions activity step for conference organizers. In bold, the aspects that were problematic because the organizers, overloaded by technical support tasks, could not perform them properly.

bold the nature of the impacted social task, which is itself a line in the activity grid of the organizers.

Figure 8 shows only one extract of the activity grid for the 'conference organizer'. There were also other participants, presenters, tech support personnel, student helpers, involved, but I will not go into the detail, in order to keep the example short. The full table for the organizer, at that level of description, counted dozens of lines.

The recommendations, among other things,[2] consisted in (1) improving the onboarding session protocol at the beginning of the conference, to ensure everything was OK with the participants and test the key functions, (2) make technical testing available online to participants long before the conference, and suggest making technical personnel support available *before* the conference starts. We also (3) provided communication back channels, some for interaction with the users, and some dedicated to organizers and tech personnel only. In sum, our intervention targeted the affordances of the VR platform, the competencies of the support personnel, the competencies of the attendees, the rules of organization for the conference staff and for the attendees ('test equipment before the conference', 'use back channels for communication if you are stuck'). This makes the whole installation more resilient and improves the satisfaction of platform users by better fulfilling one of their motives (informal networking). And, of course, intercontinental VR conferences can be more sustainable, as they produce less carbon footprint than in-person attendance.

Note here that a mere change in the order in which the actions take place has far-reaching consequences. Putting the onboarding and equipment test before the beginning of the conference unlocks resources.

Another example of such far-reaching consequences: finance decisions are crucial for the development of sustainable businesses worldwide. But, in the current decision-making process of banks, the first decision of 'which projects to consider for funding' is based on a financial, return-on-investment, appraisal of interest. Sustainability check occurs downstream in the process, when the staff have already invested time and are committed to the project and the client, as my student Annabel Ross discovered. Just as in the example of not liking the menu at the restaurant, turning back at this stage of the process is difficult. Doing the sustainability check *before* the financial assessment of interest would probably change which projects are funded, and have planetary impact. The same goes for many political decisions, which are *first* screened based on their potential impact on the popularity and career of the decision-makers.

For the sake of brevity, I have spared the reader the various activity tables. Some were long and detailed. But, in practice, full explicit detail is really necessary to communicate precisely with the installers (here, software designers and managers). If you want to best use their intelligence, you should give them not just the specifications but also the rationale for those specifications.

As one can see, designing intervention to improve an installation in a complex setting is not difficult, but it does take time, effort and discussions. You may be tempted to skip the phase of precise description with the activity grids. Resist that temptation. These grids are worth it because they will be your reference not just for implementing interventions this time, but also to document your interventions, current and future. These grids will come in handy to explain to your sponsors or stakeholders what you have done and why. It is amazing how quickly we can forget the rationale of what we have done, if we do not document it. Skilled changemakers document in detail what they do. The grids will also facilitate collaborative work because it is unlikely that you do all this by yourself.

Finally, as this specific intervention will address only a few steps in the activity (there is only so much one can do at a time!), this grid will remind you of what remains to be done for future interventions.

In practice, there are as many ways to fill in an activity grid as there are methods to follow a user in their activity. My group uses head-mounted miniature video cameras ('sub-cams') worn by users themselves as they use the installation. Later, users comment on their activity trajectory at each step (motives, goals, feelings, the relevant components, etc.) as we watch their first-person perspective recording[3] with them and ask them questions.

User shadowing, or on-site observation, can also achieve this. One thing to remember though: the activity analysis cannot be done from your office or by merely interviewing people away from the situation. It must be done by collecting data on-site, by following actual users. What people say they do is not exactly what they do. Furthermore, only on the ground can you actually fully experience the setting, with its affordances and all the rest of it. Interventions designed without detailed field observation lack realism; they are a recipe for failure because the devil is in the detail. Talk with users, employees, maintenance personnel: they know by experience what should be improved, often better than managers. Do not hesitate to use their clever ideas even if they are not yours. As a result, you will get the final credit for a better installation.

Ideally, we should consider all types of participants to the performance. This includes the contributors to the installation, such as salespersons of a shop, nurses of a hospital, civil servants of an administration and, more generally, the vast array of employees, clerks, managers, and other 'professionals'. Experience shows that personnel in charge of the maintenance are especially interesting to involve in the design process. They are best placed to know what goes wrong in the current installation and see things hidden from the top; therefore, one single interview with maintenance personnel may yield more useful knowledge than dozens of questionnaires with end-users.

Not all users are helpful for design. I recommend involving distinct types of users at each stage. In the early phase, involve 'friendly users'; those who are already convinced the change could be useful, and are happy to help.[4] The local folks will usually be able to indicate those users who are knowledgeable, smart and happy to help. Then, involve 'standard' users once the project is sufficiently advanced, once friendly users have helped you to design something that can fly. Otherwise, it is likely that standard users will just point at the obvious flaws of your design.

Remember to do things *with* the users, not *for* them. Some influential theorists of organizational change advise consultants and managers to form a coalition, and then lead the change for the rest of the organization. This tends to create an 'us vs them' dynamic that is conflict-laden, and encourages seeing resistance as something to be overcome rather than as the natural concern of the targeted stakeholders. Rather, listen and hear what stakeholders say. Changemakers have two ears and one mouth; they should listen twice as much as they talk. The motives of participants will be the engine of the future installation. You must find, with them, the way to plug these motives into your installation. Your aim is to set up the proper formal contracts and more generally the social contracts with stakeholders to ensure that their contribution is sufficiently rewarded.

This brings us to the issue of business models and socio-economic platforms, which you should consider in deciding which issues to address in your intervention, and with whom you will implement them.

11

Fixing business models and socio-economic platforms

In the course of their activity, subjects interact with others; they make transactions where things are exchanged that get parties closer to their goals and satisfy their motives. Good interactions should be at least satisficing for all participants, transactions should provide value to each party. For example, the provider/client contract ensures that the exchange of goods or services is fair, and that the giver gets compensation from the taker, while what is given matches what is promised.

When entering an installation, you consent to the social contracts that apply locally, with the expectation that this will provide you with satisfaction; e.g. when entering the restaurant, you expect to be treated as a client, and consent to behave as such. This has a ratchet effect; that is why leaving the restaurant before taking a meal is problematic: that would be a breach of social contract.

Good installations enable the users to fulfil their motives. End-users are rewarded by satisfaction (e.g. they get food, service, care) so their motives are clear. Installations mobilize not only end-users, but also a number of other parties (employees, suppliers, etc.) who contribute to the operation of the installation. These other parties are also rewarded, in different currencies. This can be money, provided by users in exchange for their satisfaction (as in market economies), but also other currencies such as access, esteem, skills. These are obtained in the social exchange processes involved in the operation of the installation. For example, in this public hospital, nurses are rewarded for their care through pay and professional pride; medical interns provide medical assistance and receive training; visitors bring comfort to patients and receive information, social and moral reward.

Usually, an installation operates in conjunction with other installations in a larger socio-economic 'platform' where activities take place. For example, a supermarket consists of several installations: the aisles, the checkout, the specialized areas such as the fishmonger's, the car park, the warehouse, and so on. Each local installation deals with a section or step of the activities that take place on that platform.

A socio-economic platform (SEP) is an organization (e.g. a clinic, a factory, a home) that brings together interested parties and organizes interaction between them by housing the relevant installations (e.g. reception, assembly line). The SEP is a place where participants can collect resources through transactions. The SEP pools resources by making each participant a provider of some of the resources needed (contribution). And the SEP enables transactions with its installations, where each participant contributes. The end result is a multi-sided social exchange, where participants make a contribution and receive a reward. The contribution and the reward can be in different currencies. For example, in this supermarket we see consumers getting products in exchange for money, employees giving work in exchange for pay and social security, trainees giving work in exchange for training. And so on.

There are many types of platforms, so the term 'organization' should be used in its broader sense. An organization is a system with a purpose. Like any system, it is made up of subsystems that are interrelated, and it is this interrelationship that enables the system to be maintained as it is, with some resilience. But an organization does not just strive to maintain its existence, rather its primary essence is (and should remain) its purpose (e.g. maintaining a state of things, transforming raw materials into useful products, providing services).

To this end, the organization establishes a series of social contracts between its subsystems (its organs: divisions, departments, etc.). In essence, the organization groups people and resources locally into its functional subsystems (the organs), each of which, as an organ, is assigned specific roles and statuses (social contracts). Together, these organs strive to achieve the organization's purpose. Organizations integrate smaller units to take their agency to the next level. Organizations are the key to addressing issues at the societal level, they are agency multipliers. By pooling forces and resources from the micro to the meso or from the meso to the macro, they make it possible to do things that the smaller units (individuals, small businesses, communities, . . .) would not be able to do. Platforms are the physical manifestation of organizations, where the action takes place.

Some platforms are very structured and are a single legal entity, e.g. a hospital, a shop, a night club, a video game. Others are still a functional organization, but may have no independent legal entity, e.g. a train station, the village square; others may even only exist in a transient manner, such as a flea market, a rave party, a beach contest – but they nevertheless are very functional organizations. What matters is that participants know their respective roles and bring to the platform what is necessary for mutually beneficial transactions. The beauty of the platform is that what each participant contributes to produce comes out to be a reward for other participants; so, overall, everyone gets some form of return for their contribution. *Platforms are the natural framework of socio-economic transactions.* Platforms do not necessarily coincide with what law considers as a unit, nor with what economics considers as an economic agent. The changemaker should consider the system in which she is intervening as a SEP; this will help to identify all the currencies potentially involved in the transactions.

Classic economics has limited its study to transactions that involve money, but we should not be limited by this restrictive approach and should consider platforms in their full extension, because we need to involve participants who are rewarded in other currencies (e.g. fame, access, social positions). And we need to factor in the contributions and rewards provided in these non-monetized currencies. For example: in this charity, volunteers provide care and get esteem and social positions; mentoring pensioners are happy to give time, of which they have too much on their hands; interns provide work and get training and academic credits. In this music club, bands come to give music and get an audience. And so on. Commercial firms are one form of platform studied by economics, but there are many others, such as family homes, public parks, ski resorts, mosques, schools, ports, street markets, power stations, shopping malls and, of course, many kinds of digital platforms. If we want to look at economic life in its entirety, we need to look at SEPs, not just companies and markets. It is in this perspective that the changemaker must design the social contracts that sustain the installations.

The drive for participation is interest, the expectancy of a satisfaction or reward. The reward can be in any currency that feeds motives (e.g. food, fame, sociability, kudos, moral relief, pleasure, knowledge). In the process, participants exchange diverse currencies. Money, because it is a generic exchange currency, is often involved in the transactions that take place on platforms, but not always and not solely. What matters for the operation of platforms, and their sustainability, is that participants get satisfaction, or at least perform satisficing transactions, and get rewarded in currencies that match their motives. The deal, formal or informal, that connects the contribution to the reward is a form of social contract.

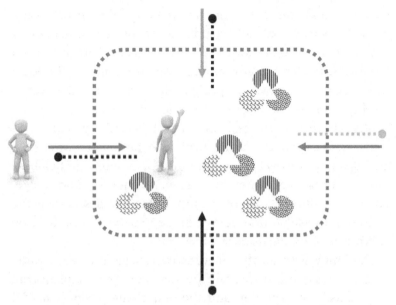

Figure 9 Platforms bring together stakeholders. Then the stakeholders' interactions are channelled by local installations to produce transactions.

There are many types of contracts. At work, specialists distinguish between *prescribed work* for which there is a formal contract and *actual work*, for which there is a 'psychological contract'.[1] The psychological differs from a formal contract because it is more flexible; e.g. while your work contract says you must work from 9am to 5pm, the psychological contract says that in case of need you are expected to stay a bit longer but, on the other hand, if you have a doctor's appointment you may leave early. For platforms, the best is to use the notion of social contract, as we defined it, which determines the respective behaviours of all parties involved, the combination of a role and a status. By consenting to the social contract, you accept a role and a corresponding status, which is the set of behaviours you will be involved in ('you do this, you get that'). Every participant in a platform has a social contract. Some also have a formal contract, some a psychological contract, some both. The social contract includes those and encompasses all the expectations on both sides. Only parts of it may be written because it includes many implicit requirements of the local (how to dress, to move, to speak, politeness rules, and so on).

The notions of socio-economic platforms and social contracts are a more realistic way of describing real-world transactions than the usual limited economistic way; they also open up a world of possibilities for sustainable business models using very different currencies (access, knowledge, fame, sociability, etc.). For example, this enables benefitting from resources that do not cost money, such as work done by volunteers or by the users themselves.

Designing with all the relevant currencies that have value for the participants makes the journey more rewarding overall for the user or customer, and the underlying business model more competitive for the provider. As gyms have understood, making the practice of physical exercise collective also leverages group belonging and emulation as motives. And, if it is too difficult to compensate for the loss of attractiveness with a positive currency, it is always possible to consider using regulation by law or channelling with affordances to make other options difficult or impossible.

When we build installations, we must make sure that they will be inserted in a platform that rewards all contributors, that it has an underlying business model that will make it sustainable. It is therefore necessary to understand what the current social contracts in currency are before we design the implementation, to assess if the new contracts will be acceptable by the interested parties. Those who lose in the change will be likely to resist unless they get fair compensation, while those who will gain might become allies in implementing the change and making it sustainable. We shall see in the design and implementation process how to factor these currencies and contracts into the analysis.

12

Choosing issues, moments, and stakeholders

Once you have completed the activity grid, you can use its lines to identify steps that are problematic for all or some users or stakeholders – for example, steps that are risky, cause failures, or are inaccessible to special needs. They could also be steps that cause problems external to the installation itself: externalities such as pollution, political issues, resource depletion, social damage.

Now comes the moment of choosing which issues to tackle. This choice has two sides: what should ideally be done (the importance of the issue) and what you can realistically do (your agency). Building material affordances is expensive; building competence implies having access to users; building regulation is a political issue that requires influence and power.

Issues and moments: a matter of agency

Perhaps your current agency, your own and your sponsor's, is not sufficient. If so, look at the problem from a larger perspective of which stakeholders are involved in the installation, and over a longer time frame. In this context, you can increase your

agency with allies and proceed step by step, as your intervention gains momentum. For example, when you try to improve
people's fitness, you run into a lot of practical issues, such as
transport and work schedules. It would be easier if people could
exercise close to where they work. In fact, employers have an
interest in the fitness and well-being of their employees, so why
not consider the employer as a potential stakeholder and discuss
with them the possibility of installing a gym in their facility?

Some resources or political windows that are currently
unavailable may become available later if you play your cards
right. Start with what you can do now, the 'low hanging fruit'.
This will build momentum and trigger further gains. A first
successful implementation will earn the trust of stakeholders
and win you allies.

In the early days of video-conferencing, my team faced a
lot of resistance from the IT division of our company; they
were afraid that installing such a system would overload the
networks and cause them to collapse. But, after we managed
to install it at European sites of the R&D division, which was
more open to innovation, the board realized how convenient
and reliable it was, and we gained enough top-level support
to get the go-ahead for the whole company. And then, as we
became more trusted, we started to introduce bolder and
bolder innovations. As the Arab saying goes, 'First you work
for your reputation, then your reputation works for you.'

The trust you gain even in easy success is justified. As Kurt
Lewin said, the best way to understand a system is to try to
change it. So, you actually increase your knowledge of the
system and the way it works (politically, technically, etc.) as
you implement interventions. Finally, your own belief in your
capacity to change the local system (your 'self-efficacy'), and
your increased knowledge of the system, will increase your
agency and self-efficacy for the next step.

As you review the list of pain points, consider which components in each layer could create the desired channelling,

and assess whether you actually have the agency to implement them. Then look at the bigger picture. Who would be best placed to implement them? Which of the current stakeholders? Are there other entities (people, organizations, governments, media, unions, foundations, etc.) that have the necessary resources to fill some layer? What are their motives? Would it be possible to establish the right social contracts with them so that they contribute their resources? Discuss this with them. Remember that a platform lives on the resources brought in by others; do not limit your imagination to your own resources. For example, it turns out that an effective way to get adults to change their behaviour at home (e.g. turning off lights when not in use, sorting rubbish) is to get their children to act as vigilantes. Children are motivated by a sustainable future. By educating children at school, you are introducing and enforcing good adult practice at home. (Don't go too far, however, as some dictatorial regimes have done by using children as informers.)

Resistance to change is natural, but not insurmountable. Remember that what is unacceptable now may seem acceptable in the future if stakeholders are given enough time to prepare. Look at how governments implemented tough regulations banning certain fuels (e.g. coal, diesel), chemicals (e.g. pesticides) or vehicles (e.g. internal combustion engines): they gave stakeholders several years to prepare. Set implementation dates in the future so that people can prepare. You may not want to accept the changes for yourself, but you can agree that your successors can accept the new contract; this has been done to remove some privileges. The change can also be introduced as an 'experiment', to be evaluated in a year or so, with the promise of a return to the previous state if unsatisfactory. 'Experiments' are more acceptable than final decisions; they are also harder to argue against.

If there is a flow or cycle (e.g. seasonal), implement the change with a new wave of users. It takes a full cycle to become 'the way we do things around here'. Do not be discouraged if it does not work at first. Even if the newcomers are not aware that this is a new installation and are willing to accept it as 'the way we do things', the previous staff or users still know the previous version and may question the legitimacy of the new 'way we do things'. But, once the change has started, it has its own momentum and people are likely to follow.

Do not seek perfection. Implementation is a matter of solving crossed constraints, so it will be a trade-off. If those who lose in the trade-off are properly compensated, resistance will diminish. An installation is a living device; in use it will gradually improve as participants creatively modify it and users embody the relevant competencies. Ultimately, changemakers are judged on the quality of their trade-offs, and perfection is not expected.

It is important to find the right place to implement the components and the right time to implement the change. When considering where to implement, always remember the principle of channelling at the point of action. If your intervention requires changing a layer, choose a time when the targets are available for change. For affordances, a good window is when equipment needs to be replaced due to obsolescence. For people, a window of opportunity is when they are open to rethinking their current practice and have the mental space to do so. This is why car sellers send prospective messages to car owners when they know their car is starting to age, by using the list of number plates. It is also why utility companies are particularly aggressive in marketing to people when they move to a new home. And so on.

Robust installations are multilayered and building them takes time. Consider emergency care for heart attacks. Countries that installed defibrillators in many public places and pharmacies and trained the population in first aid and performing artificial respiration have seen a reduction in the number of heart-attack deaths. Here the installation is distributed among the population, in the environment and in institutions, with the training of specialized emergency personnel and their phone numbers, procedures, status, priority in traffic for ambulances, and so on. These successful installations are the result of analyses of the steps to be taken in the event of a heart attack, carried out progressively over the years.

Stakeholder analysis and involvement

Stakeholder analysis is essential if you want your intervention to have a lasting effect. Stakeholders can be resources or obstacles. List them and their motives as you encounter them when filling in the activity grid. Suppose you are following a particular type of stakeholder (e.g. the consumer) step by step: you can list all the stakeholders as they enter the scene to contribute to the activity. Just think about who brings resources or controls the activity at each step. This will bring out the different types of employees of the installation, its owners, the local authorities, competitors, organizations in charge of procurement, maintenance, regulation, repair, control, and so on. Think of all the stakeholders to be taken into account in the example of the management of heart attacks, from bystanders to the intensive care units, but also all the administrative staff involved, down to those in charge of the regular checks of the defibrillators.

Let us take an example where the use of some dormant stakeholders (the bystanders) as vigilantes contributed to the success of a difficult intervention. The city of Barrancabermeja (at the time, a town of 100,000 inhabitants in Colombia, mostly active in the oil industry) had a rising rate of domestic violence in the early 2000s, higher than the rest of the country. A multilayered intervention was able to halt and reverse this trend (Figure 10).

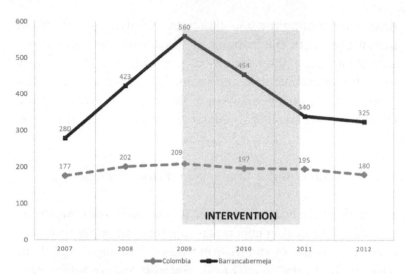

Figure 10   Recorded cases of domestic violence in
Barrancabermeja and Columbia (documented lesions, fatal or not:
cases per 100,000 inhabitants). Source: Instituto Nacional de
Medicina Legal (Forensis), 2007–12. In Barrancabermeja, after the
intervention, in two years the rate went down from 560 to 340 per
100,000.

How was it done?

An analysis of domestic violence deaths (almost all femini-
cides) showed that jealousy was often the triggering motive.
The local macho culture and the social acceptance of violence
made aggression and violent behaviour the 'natural' solution,
a solution that was considered 'normal' or at least acceptable
by the neighbourhood. This led to many violent episodes (over
500 per year at the beginning of the intervention) and a high
number of deaths.

The intervention[1] combined actions on the three layers,
addressing one of the motives (jealousy) by setting up a
'jealous anonymous' telephone line, where jealous men could
call and get counselling before resorting to violence. This
physical intervention was combined with building the competence to use it. Using an approach initiated by Antanas Mockus'

group, 'invisible theatre' sessions were organized in the street (where the public is unaware that this is theatre and not a real scene): a couple were arguing in the street and, when a crowd gathered around and the argument started to get violent, another comedian disguised as a giant telephone arrived on the scene and explained to the crowd that the argument had been staged to make them aware of the use of this anonymous jealousy hotline and distribute red referee 'whistles against abuse'.

An event with authorities and celebrities pledging to end domestic violence was held, well-known artists were invited to include songs against violence in their albums, which were then broadcast on the scene and on the radio. Journalists were trained, home visits were made. Finally, ten thousand 'whistles against abuse' were distributed to enable neighbours to whistle if they heard or saw domestic violence, and potential victims to call for help. The intervention thus targeted critical points of orientation in men's behaviour in order to inhibit or stop the process of activity that led to episodes of violence. More importantly, by creating proper affordances and channelling, it gave different actors (potential victims and perpetrators, passers-by, authorities, family members, journalists . . .) easier, safer, more 'acceptable' ways to act in a complex, unpredictable situation, in which many people would opt for inaction.

This example, described in more detail by my student and colleague Paulius Yamin,[2] is interesting because it shows that a multilayered approach can change behaviour to make the world a better place, not only on the environmental and economic pillars of sustainability, but also on the social pillar. It should be noted that although the above intervention applied the principles of installation theory and multilayered installation design, it did not explicitly use them, as the theory had not yet been published! Societies and wise changemakers have been using these design principles for centuries, even before they were formalized. But using the activity grid greatly facilitates the design of interventions.

It is important to identify the motives and values of stake-holders in order to construct social contracts with them. Here it is useful to have understood the motives of the stakeholders and also how their specific activity relates to the SEP's business model (e.g. the hospital, the street, the neighbourhood, the city). This will influence the choice of which component to install, which stakeholder to involve, and with which social contract. In the examples of Mockus' interventions, the social contract is the civic contract of membership of a community and demands fundamental ethical values such as the protection of life and care for fellow human beings.

In other cases, the contract may be more instrumental. For example, if you want to have a helpdesk at your conference, you will have to pay for it with money, unless you can find people willing to do the work for some other kind of reward. Many scientific conferences use unpaid student volunteers who are interested in demonstrating their commitment to the scientific organizers, as well as getting free access to information and useful networking. You can only expect a sustainable contribution from stakeholders if they find their interest in participating, if they have a fair social contract.

Since, in practice, an installation has a considerable number of stakeholders, you will often limit your detailed stakeholder analysis to the steps in which you intervene. Even then, there are many. How many stakeholders should you consider, and how far should you go? Users and employees, maintenance staff, of course. Major suppliers, perhaps. Regulators? Maybe. There is no hard and fast answer to the question of how many – it is another of those 'how long is a piece of string' questions. The answer is 'enough for your purpose'.

The general principle of intervention is to work with the system rather than against it, and to enrol as many forces as possible. This means that sometimes you have to take a step-by-step approach, waiting for stakeholders to see that things are moving so that they are convinced. The best argument is to show, with concrete examples or demonstrations, that the new installation works; this is much more effective than trying to convince with documents or plans. In the video-conferencing example I gave above, the top management was not convinced by plans or projects, but only when they saw the pilot installation working.

Convincing some key stakeholders is useful in three ways. First, you suppress resistance; second, you win allies. Third, the fact that you have convinced some important characters such as leaders will make it easier to convert other people to trust you, because people tend to imitate their leaders. Sometimes you will only get neutrality at first: that is better than opposition. The more you progress, the more your initiative will gain momentum. For this reason, the timing of your implementation will be difficult to predict. There will be moments of delay and moments of acceleration. Be patient and persistent in the moments of delay, be bold and decisive in the moments of acceleration.

13

Multilayered Installation Design

Finding the right intervention, which components to change or implement, is a gradual process. Most often the first idea will not work perfectly, because the change introduced will get in the way of the activity of another participant or be problematic for an external stakeholder whom you had not noticed. That is why your intervention plans should be discussed with stakeholders. Proposed solutions often raise new problems. As they are abandoned, or as the new problems are tackled, the actors are put in creative mode; they can focus on motives and change their goals. It is a dialectic progression that may end in a quite different place than participants initially thought.

The power of discussion

In the discussion, suggesting intervention in various layers opens new perspectives to participants; new motives and new goals can appear. As in the example of the shower, simply changing the sequence of the steps, and who does what, may allow for a new distribution of tasks and make untapped resources available. Taking the problem from different perspectives, and looking at the big picture, allows participants to see the issue differently, outside of the original box. This discussion phase is important because it takes some time, brings in new information and allows participants, especially those who are initially reluctant or sceptical, to open up to new views and perhaps change their attitude without losing face.

In which layers should you intervene? That depends on your agency. If you have a budget, affordances are usually a layer that raises minimal resistance. If you have user access, you can work directly on competencies. If you have political leverage (or, in an organization, managerial leverage), regulation is a powerful instrument. Consider all layers and remember that other stakeholders might bring in the desired components if you find a social contract that satisfies their motives. Do not start from what you can do; start from the problem, and consider what you would do if you had unlimited budget and agency. Then explore if there exists some stakeholder who would have an interest in providing that component. Only if you find none, or no possibility of involving them, then go to your own resources.

A question I am often asked is whether such or such component is in this or that layer. It does not matter as long as that component channels in the way you want. There is no such thing as a component purely in a single layer anyway. Reality is a continuous fabric, we do need conceptual instruments to cut it into individualized phenomena that we can work with (components, layers); but the cut is always somewhat artificial. The model is just a representation of the reality, not reality itself ('the map is not the territory'). Do not worry, and focus on finding solutions; the three-layer framework is just there to make sure you look in all the right directions to search for effective components in the various dimensions of affordances (physical realm), competencies (psychological realm) and regulation (social realm). The same about installations: 'Is this an installation or part of an installation? Is the train or the train station an installation?' Never mind: what you want is to design devices that channel behaviour and, in practice, they all connect to one another as the activity deploys: their core is clear, but their limits can be blurry.

A lot of these issues will clarify in discussion; dealing with things in practice is often simpler than trying to find a solution in theory.

Evaluation, correction and deployment

After these explorations and discussions, when a promising intervention design is finally selected, an implementation trial is carried out. It needs to be carefully monitored and treated as what it is: a proof of concept and a first attempt. Often at this stage, new issues arise that need to be addressed. Often it is only at this stage that we become aware of the existence of distant stakeholders. This is because the installation, or some of its components, are also involved in activities other than the one under consideration and have an impact elsewhere. For example, you may implement a new procurement system that satisfies the accountants but drives some departments crazy, or vice versa; or satisfies both but drives the suppliers crazy.

Often the devil is in the detail – but that detail has far-reaching organizational implications. For example, you realize that you had not anticipated that someone should be responsible for ensuring that the batteries in the security equipment are charged, but this is not in anyone's job description, and you have to negotiate with HR. Fair enough. Just repeat the analysis, fix it with the three layers and test again until it works. There will be several iterations before deployment, unless you are lucky.

It is essential to include in the design of an installation its maintenance process and the possibility of its evolution. This applies to affordances, but also to the other layers. In particular, it is important to specify who is responsible for deciding on changes and who will pay for them. These are classic design issues, but the multilayered installation framework proves helpful here.

14

Tips for the changemaker

Intervention design is both an art and a science. I have described here the way my group and I have done it so far, but every situation is different; there is no single best way. You should adapt to your own situation, the problem at hand and your agency. In your interventions, you should apply the classic rules of the trade and good practice of organizational change, action research or intervention, depending on the institutional framework in which you operate. Our approach, with its specific emphasis on user involvement and systematic three-layered design, brings some issues to the fore. Here are some lessons learned from practice. You may find them helpful.

Decision and vision

Before changing behaviour, it is fair to clarify how and why the decision to change is made. For example, should we ban private transport? What uses of this or that technology (e.g. biometrics, gene editing) should be encouraged or banned? etc. These questions may seem intractable in general, because people have different opinions and interests. Fortunately, in local practice, at the level of the changemaker, the problem looks different and is usually solvable. The big decisions, the ones that require political compromise, are usually already taken at the political level, and then the behaviour change intervention is mostly a problem of practical implementation.

However, these remote decisions may have overlooked important aspects. The changemaker should never hesitate to go back to the decision-makers and sponsors and discuss if it turns out that their decision missed a crucial point. New aspects of the problem often emerge as you get into the details of implementation, and this may require a rethink of the whole intervention. For example, you may discover that your intervention on more fuel-efficient vehicles has rebound effects (e.g. people drive more as a result).

As a changemaker, you have some responsibility for the changes you implement, and you should think before you act (remember the chapter on ethics). The fact that you have been asked to do this or that is no excuse. Throughout history, changemakers have implemented concentration camps. They implemented well what were evil instructions: doing well is not always doing good. Use your moral and social judgement. A responsible changemaker should always take a moment to reflect on his or her own motives before designing interventions. Reflexivity is about zooming back on the whole situation until the changemaker herself appears in the big picture. What is the relationship between the changemaker and the target system? On whose behalf, why and for whom is the changemaker acting? What values are involved? This zooming back reminds the changemaker of his or her responsibility to society, over and above the contract that binds him or her to the sponsor of the intervention.

Do not hesitate to go to higher levels of the organization when you encounter an ethical issue. Always remember that the rules at one level are only parameters at the higher level, so if you get support at the right level of power or hierarchy, your task will be made easier. Often your intervention will be resisted at intermediate levels of power because it disrupts their routine; but the purpose of your intervention may be supported by higher levels who can help you resolve this resistance. Different societies and organizations have different ways of making political decisions; it is certainly easier to use these processes than to confront them. But one thing that remains constant in all organizations is that allies and networks are especially important, often more important than the rules. If you go to the right level of the organization, rules can be changed, or an exception can be made.

Most interventions are minor changes, an evolution of an existing subsystem. They appear as channelling slightly different trajectories for a given activity, some kind of gradual 'betterment' of the system, locally. Change can be implemented incrementally, starting with fixing problems as they arise, in a design loop that analyses the problem, tests a solution with users, and iterates until a new satisfactory regime is found. Interestingly, while one might think that such a step-by-step method could only produce minor changes, it turns out that radical evolutions can sometimes happen in the process. Society is like a large boat: it cannot make sharp turns, but if it turns long enough it can change direction completely. Look at how people have adapted to the ban on smoking in public places, to wearing seat belts in cars, etc. The way we work has changed massively with modern technologies. Away from crisis situations, it is easier to get people to change a little than a lot; but many little changes can go a long way.

Diversity and resistance

Not everyone will be happy with adopting the new behaviour we are trying to channel. There is usually resistance from those (the majority) who prefer to keep to the old ways, since humans are creatures of habit. This is especially true if the new behaviour requires efforts, if one must throw away equipment or status: 'Why should I use the stairs rather than the elevator? Why should we promote minorities?' etc.

Resistance is useful for the changemaker because it reveals pain points that should be resolved. The useful resistance is the one that is vocal and expresses its reasons for dissent ('voice').[1] In the case of silent resistance, the changemaker should elicit users' voice, discuss with those who resist to understand their reasons, and listen to the alternative solutions they put forward, which are sometimes better than the initial plan.

The issue of accessibility and special needs is trickier. A basic principle of a good society is that every loyal member should be able to proceed with the activities they need to perform. But some people have special needs, for example they may have a specific characteristic that prevents them from performing the target behaviour: people in wheelchairs will not climb stairs, foreigners cannot read the local language, babies do not fit in the car seat, vegetarians will not eat meat, etc. The principle is that you should strive to make the installation flexible enough for diverse people to use comfortably, which is the hallmark of advanced societies. Then, of course, there is also a trade-off with complexity and cost.

More generally, it is difficult to set up an installation that caters for everyone with the exact same satisfaction, because people have diverse characteristics and motives. It is true that most classic cultural installations appear to manage to fit everyone's needs, but remember that it took many trials and errors to reach their current efficient specifications. For example, how high and wide a seat, or a door, should be. Furthermore, there has been adaptation of the users, who have been conditioned to act in the proper way and find this behaviour normal. And these installations are deeply multilayered: road traffic is regulated by roundabouts, road signs, but also by driving licences which involve serious training.

Rather than designing the whole installation to be able to accommodate for all rare cases, it is often easier, and more efficient, to construct an extra installation to cater specifically for some special needs. Take wheelchair accessibility. It might turn out impossible, especially in the case of old buildings, to make each room accessible to wheelchairs on a permanent basis. But protocols can be installed to address in a transient manner the rare cases where a person in a wheelchair needs to access one of these rooms that are not designed for wheelchair access. You can use other layers than the affordances of the environment, and especially other humans. A movable ramp can be installed, the person can be carried up the stairs by two robust helpers with a suitable device. Another example: if some users have a special diet, offer a variety of dishes rather than imposing this diet on all users in the cafeteria.

The conclusion is: do not hesitate to design several distinct installations to cater for diversity, rather than designing a single one that risks being one-size-poorly-fits-all, or becoming convoluted and difficult to operate and maintain.

Editing the default option

Once a behaviour is learned, it can become a default option. As we saw, making sure the subjects learn the proper default option is especially important. Default options can be changed if the subject is driven into considering anew their behaviour. That motivation generally comes from perceived dissonance between what the subject usually does and what she perceives as appropriate. For example, if the conditions have changed and the current behaviour is not appropriate anymore, like when moving home, where a lot of routines must change.

Another case is when the current behaviour produces failure and leads the subject to reconsider, as when taking improper care of a plant causes its decay. Change can also come from social feedback, as when someone is told what to wear in a specific occasion. All these are 'windows of opportunity' for behavioural change.[2] For individuals, changes in circumstances such as marriage, having children, widowhood, moving house, changing jobs, illness are such windows. For communities, moments of rapid growth or crises are windows of opportunity. This is why it is said that crises are also opportunities, and this is certainly true for behaviour change. The crisis provides the changemaker the 'unfreeze' that facilitates change. But remember that a crisis will be an opportunity to change only if an alternative solution is readily available. That is why it is good to prepare, and sometimes you will have to wait for the window of opportunity.

But the most effective approach is to modify behaviour at the time when habits are formed. This may mean early in life. Here is an example of how interventions can change behaviour into better habits. Adequate water intake is essential, and drinking sugary drinks at an early age is thought to contribute to obesity and diabetes later in life because it becomes a habit. It is therefore important that children's drinking habits include adequate water intake and minimize sugary drinks if we are to halt the obesity epidemics.

The intervention[3] consisted of a randomized control trial in which the design provided families with information (to change the embodied competencies of parents and children), affordances (in the form of small 'child-sized' water bottles delivered free to the home) and some social regulation (by creating an online forum where parents could share their experiences). The intervention took place in Poland, where children had a low hydration status and a high consumption of sugary drinks compared to the rest of Europe.

Families with children aged three to six were followed for one year and their drinking was monitored six times during the year, in one-week waves, to assess short and long-term effects. In total 343 participants stayed until the end of the experiment (30% dropped out). Detailed behaviour was also recorded by asking some volunteer mothers to record their day with wearable miniature video cameras. In short, the results show a significant increase in water consumption, an increase that becomes more important as more layers are involved in the intervention (although the social layer had little impact here, as most parents were lurkers rather than active in the online forum).

At the peak of the intervention, when families were simultaneously exposed to the three layers, information, the forum and the delivery of water bottles to their homes, the average daily water consumption of the child was almost three times higher than in the control group (343 ml vs. 128 ml). Analysis of all intake data shows that this extra water consumption was actually a substitution for sugary drinks, which were consumed less. So, the intervention was very successful.

However, when the affordances (the small bottles) were removed, the magnitude of the effect decreased. The difference remained highly significant, with consumption almost twice as high as in the control group, but still not as high as before. The explanation is obvious: since the behaviour is the result of the different components, removing one of them (in this case the water bottles) reduces the effect.

Interestingly, six months after the end of the intervention, the effect of the three-layered intervention was still significant because the families had acquired new habits and a better taste for water. Qualitative analysis of the videotapes with the mothers showed that just seeing the water bottles reminded them to drink. The tapes also showed the strong social regulation of mothers encouraging their children to drink water instead of sugary drinks, influenced by the information they had received and the tips they had exchanged with other parents. Naturally, such an intervention is not enough to stop the obesity epidemic on its own, but adding interventions that address each step where bad habits are formed helps. And, of course, interventions on the supply side (the food industry, canteens) could gradually help to solve the problem.

Integration in the larger system

Interventions for change face a problem that is classic in innovation: the integration within the larger system. Society was never a blank slate where every local behaviour is independent from others and from the past. So, whatever behaviour you want to implement, expect that there are already behaviours that fulfil a similar function. Because the same human functions have always been around (transport, education, health care, etc.), and are catered for. Your intervention will have to take this installed basis into account.

This 'installed basis' has good and bad sides. The good side is that users already have embodied skills for all the steps of the new process that are similar to the previous. And the same goes with the other layers: rules, tools, and even the other people and organizations involved in the previous installation are still there, and they can be used as components of the new installation. Some competencies, rules, artefacts, and stakeholders in other installations can also be imported into the new, just as one would reconstruct a new figure using Lego bricks. For example, people can read and so can their smart devices, therefore new installations can use natural language, graphic or magnetic codes, etc., to communicate with users and make transactions; a new type of individual vehicle will still likely have seats, lights, and a driving wheel. Society already educates people with the appropriate skills for standard roles. So you can easily build your new installation with these standard components that fit into known social contracts for which all the social, technical, legal and administrative apparatus is available off the shelf.

On the other hand, the bad side comes from exactly the same issue: users already have embodied skills that may be at odds with what is needed for the new path. So they may resist change, or make mistakes with the new installation. You have to deal with it. Use the existing components when you can, import those you can from other installations, change the rest. One important thing to remember, though, is that it is exceedingly difficult to change a system from the outside only, as someone who fights it. It is always handy to have allies within the system who will help you from the inside – e.g. 'confederates' who share the same vision, ideology, interests, or simply friends. Find and cultivate these allies.

Of course, there is also a need to intervene on the supply side, which drives the culture of growth and consumption. Industry complains that it would if it could, but it is locked into a competitive system and if it produces more sustainably it will not survive. Mostly, they are sincere. This is because they are still thinking in terms of the classical economy of goods and services – and not in terms of SEP – hence neglecting the deeper motives of their customers, who are social animals interested not only in comfort and convenience but also in belonging, recognition, self-improvement and all the things that come from social relationships. As what matters for consumers is overall satisfaction, it is possible to compensate for a lower worth of one value (e.g. usability) with worth in another value (e.g. social reward, future benefits). The example of smartphones, a highly competitive industry that, like most electronics industries, is engaged in a mad race for innovation and planned obsolescence, is instructive. Here, more than anywhere else, a company that does not play the game should not survive, according to the argument above. Really?

Interestingly, one company has decided to commit to fair business practices (traceable components, fair labour contracts, etc.) and to produce phones that are more sustainable, durable and made up of modular components that consumers can easily replace themselves, thus upgrading as technology advances. These phones are more robust, a little bulkier, a little less ergonomic and a little more expensive than their competitors. But they have found a market, and the company is growing. Why is that? Perhaps because in the long run it is cheaper than buying a new phone every two years. But more importantly, buyers get the satisfaction of acting on their beliefs to help the environment and feel part of a community of like-minded people. They are rewarded in other currencies, social and moral. The company has done a good job of installation, building the skills of its users with online tutorials explaining how to change components. Replacement parts are easy, quick and cheap to get by post. And the company has built up a community of users.

There are many such examples where the price barrier has been overcome by other factors – in organic foods, fair trade goods, etc. Activity theory tells us that as long as the installation (including the product) satisfies, it is viable. Now, beyond this minimum, in terms of competition between concurrent installations (the competitor problem), what the user takes into account is overall satisfaction, and this includes all kinds of currencies, and especially the social rewards that are often neglected. The latter, as shown in the example above, can more than compensate for the material aspects of satisfaction. And social and moral aspects usually have little or no environmental footprint.

So, as a provider, or the changemaker working for a provider, think carefully about the social contract you are building with your users. As long as the product (or service) provides minimal functional satisfaction, it is the terms of the social contract that matter most. Modifying the provider's installations to fulfil a better social contract, offering social and self-enhancing benefits, is the way to survive competition while progressing towards greater sustainability.

Timing

One problem for transition is, ironically, the resilience of the current installation. The power of a crisis is to free one from the previous system's homeostatic mechanisms. It also makes the need to change salient even to those whose usual interest was to keep the system as it is. Crises are good moments for change; it may be good to plan and wait for the crisis. Then, better plan seriously because during a crisis everything will have to be done in a hurry, with little time to think. Changing the system during a crisis is, by the way, a good defence against frustration and anger: to resist successfully it is better to construct a new solution than to fight to defend the current system under attack, and action is a psychological remedy against the anxiety and grief which usually come with crises.

Apart from moments of crisis, the larger system is likely to be a source of resistance to change. But if you endeavour to change, there is a reason for this, something that does not work. So, the moments of salience of that issue are the best moments to intervene. Then the system will resist less, and you will also find interested allies and resources to support your action. For example, measures to save energy, water or money are best accepted in times of scarcity. And then these measures can be made permanent. The City of Paris has made permanent the temporary cycle lanes introduced during the 2020 Covid closure. Measures to change social practices (corruption, discrimination, exploitation, various types of misconduct) are best accepted in the wake of a scandal.

More generally, change is easier if you first 'unfreeze' the current state of things. The current situation comes with behavioural habits and default options that stand in the way of doing things differently, so destabilizing this state of affairs makes it easier to introduce new ways of doing things. Sometimes the general situation unfreezes naturally, as when a family moves, a person changes jobs or status, there is an accident or simply the need for replacement due to obsolescence; or, for larger systems, there is a crisis. Otherwise, the changemaker and his sponsor need to justify the change. This can be done by pointing out the limitations of the current installation and arguing that the change will bring an improvement according to the current values of the user community.

Going beyond Multilayered Installation Design

I have focused on the functional approach of how to signpost and channel the activity trajectory step by step, using the layers of installation theory. But changing behaviour is not only about designing the right installations. The attitude of the stakeholders to the process of change itself is important. If they are supportive, they will accept the effort and minor inconveniences that come with any change. If they are opposed, then no matter how good the changes you want to implement, you are doomed. Involving stakeholders or their representatives in the change process will help to get a critical mass of stakeholders on the side of change, or at least win their neutrality.

Gaining the support of stakeholders does not happen naturally: you must ask for help and support. That is fine because asking for help is the best way to make friends. Remember the effect of dissonance described earlier, when explaining why you are more prone to give some change to those beggars to whom you already gave the time, or some directions. In the same vein, we tend to like people we helped (interestingly, sometimes we prefer them to those people who actually helped us, because we do not like to be in debt). So, do ask stakeholders for help; not only may you get the resources you need now, but you may also gain long-term allies. It is amazing how people can become helpful when asked.

Often participants will agree with the principles underlying the intervention, so there is no deep opposition of principle, but rather there is opposition because of inconvenience. You need some force to overcome this (passive) resistance; social participation can be that force. If the intervention process becomes a social movement, then people will participate for the social movement aspect of it. That is the mechanism used for fund raising, for example: you create a social setting where people are eager to participate; and participation entails giving. Formalizing this involvement with a pledge, where participants engage publicly, is effective (remember the Lewin intervention on offal). Making the intervention a collective endeavour allows people to enjoy the warm glow of participation, and also limits the avoidance of reactance because participants take ownership. Public commitment locks people into their commitment; it also reinforces group membership, which is a powerful motivator.

There have been remarkably successful examples of creating such movements around change. In the social movement created by the British National Health Service to bring about massive organizational change, local units publicly pledged to improve their installations. Many political revolutions have exploited and orchestrated moments of public collective engagement. People like to be part of a collective effort; in groups we often go beyond what we would do alone, sometimes for the worse, but also for the better.

Among the most spectacular are the changes introduced by Antanas Mockus when he was mayor of Bogotá to reduce crime, traffic accidents, water consumption, and even make people pay voluntarily more tax.[4] Communication campaigns were used to involve citizens in the intervention process rather than trying to educate them. They raised awareness of latent motives, showed citizens their responsibility and encouraged them, with humour, to be changemakers, but also to act as vigilantes. The campaigns also turned the intervention into a public show in which everyone participated. In one famous example mentioned earlier, Mockus hired 400 mime artists to go to the city's main crossroads and gently mock drivers or pedestrians who did not respect the traffic rules. Then 350,000 thumbs-up/thumbs-down cards were distributed to the public, who could wave them in the faces of those who behaved badly (thumbs down) or well (thumbs up). Road accidents fell by half. This public intervention was so popular that it is still vivid in the collective memory of the city decades later.

Humans are a terrible species and often show themselves to be capable of the worst, especially when acting as a mass. But experience shows that, when prompted by intelligent intervention, they are also capable of collectively correcting their behaviour, and this should give us hope for the decades ahead.

Conclusion

Tools, knowledge, society: that is how we build civilizations. These three assets augment the individual human body, and their combination greatly increases human agency compared to other animals. These assets feed a virtuous cycle of societal development with division of labour, development of technology and transmission of know-how that has no equivalent in other species.

The ubiquitous installations we see today are the product and instrument of our tool-savvy, cultural and social species. Installations are the devices by which humans combine these three assets to make their lives easier. Through installations we channel our behaviour to achieve what we want or what society requires.

Installations are how people make society and contribute to its transformation. They are the bars of the golden cage that empowers and controls us.[1] So, when we design installations, we are simply doing what the human species has always done spontaneously for ages. We just do it more reflexively and systematically.

In this book we have seen the three layers of components that make up installations and how they channel behaviour:

affordances in the environment, embodied competencies and social regulation. Inspired by this, we have seen how we can become changemakers by using these components to channel behaviour through design, education and regulation.

By applying installation theory to behaviour analysis and intervention design, behavioural scientists and other researchers and practitioners, and changemakers more generally, can gain a full and coherent picture of the many layers of components that channel any given behaviour: from physical spaces and objects to knowledge and beliefs, to social norms and legal rules. While changemakers generally take some of these elements into account, they often do so in a tangential or unstructured way, where a complete picture would facilitate systemic interventions. Installation theory radically opens up the range of possible interventions. In a way that makes it easier to tackle societal and systemic challenges.

Indeed, such changes are now urgently needed, on a societal level. History has shown us that societies are plagued by a 'tragic spiral' when faced with stress: human beings tend to react to stress by acting against the cause, which is the positive way, or by escaping – if they can – or by aggression, against others or themselves (e.g. psychosomatic disorders). Alas, human beings have a sad tendency to attribute the cause of problems to someone else – a scapegoat, a stranger, an enemy or even a neighbour. And then the tragic spiral begins: stress, aggression, violence, retaliation, destruction. In this spiral, stress and destruction feed on each other until the participants are unable to continue, or until a third party intervenes to stop the spiral.

We should now turn our efforts to addressing the serious problems we have created with our irresponsible growth and use of the planet's resources, as their scarcity will inevitably create global stress. With nowhere to run and no third party to intervene, positive collective action is the only way out if we are to avoid a global tragic spiral that is likely to emerge from this global stress.

And it is feasible. We have seen how behaviours can be implemented and maintained with multilayered installation design, and how these installations can be made sustainable by linking them to the business model of the platforms that host them. Designing or redesigning an installation requires a detailed analysis of the target activity, which involves working and collaborating with users and stakeholders to understand their motivations and experiences, and listening to their ideas for improvement. It is not difficult, but it does require work, filling in activity grids, going out into the field and accepting compromises.

One can feel discouraged when considering the propensities of humans to be aggressive, selfish, competitive, xenophobic, risk averse, etc. Yes, we all are so. Do not be discouraged: remember we all host also the complementary and opposite propensities (to be caring, altruistic, collaborative, curious, etc.), they can be exploited. The smart changemaker will leverage the bright side of the psychological forces, and reward people with the warm glow.

Collaboration is good because it is more productive (big things and large scale cannot be achieved alone); it is also emotionally and socially rewarding. Undertaking change together not only benefits from collective intelligence, but also enables us to support each other through difficult times and maintain our commitment to action.

We can use installations to change behaviour at an individual level, as in the shower example. Such small changes may seem anecdotal, but a small change multiplied by billions has a big impact. We have seen from the example of smartphone obsolescence that business models can be changed to be more sustainable, and that the immense power of industry and communication can be harnessed in a positive way. Even thorny social problems that seem to require massive cultural change, such as domestic violence, can be tackled successfully. Catastrophic pandemics like Covid-19 can be overcome when governments get serious about the problem. And the interventions of Mockus and his team show that if you manage to mobilize social forces, you can achieve massive effects quickly and on a large scale. For example, during a water shortage, Mockus managed, in two months, to reduce Bogotá's water consumption by 14%, by showing in a video clip how to stop the water during the moment when you soap yourself, and later this reduction went up to 40% as people realized the savings.[2] Yes, change is possible. The fastest way to solve our energy, food or climate change problems, which are now driving us into a tragic spiral, would be to produce and consume less and more responsibly. Many social problems could be solved by changing behaviour, especially those related to the unequal distribution of resources, knowledge and labour.

Of course, these changes require strong political decisions and real investment. It is an illusion to believe that results can be achieved at low cost, without political risk, without individual effort and without some loss. The level of investment in behavioural change at national level should be comparable to that in infrastructure (transport, energy, etc.), because the key issues of our time are behavioural. Money and other resources are indeed very important; but they are not the only issues. A key question is: what do we use them for? And, by the way, remember that a skilled changemaker is one who persuades those who have the resources to use them for the right purpose.

But we should not expect governments to do all the work. In businesses, in all organizations, at an individual level, we must all make our local effort to change our practices as producers, consumers and citizens, even if the benefits are rarely immediate. We must all accept the costs of the necessary changes, or we will all feel the pain of the tragic spiral.

The social sciences and humanities have a role to play here, because people are the cause of the problems we face, and they are also the solution. The natural sciences and biology have applied their models; they feed material technology, medicine and agriculture. It is time for the social sciences and humanities to apply their knowledge to social technology. Economics, management, politics, marketing, behavioural science are examples of areas where the social sciences and humanities are already being applied to the management of human affairs, but so far mostly to support the current growth-based system, which has reached its limits. We now need to develop and apply social science to a societal technology that addresses the way we do things on this planet, as the species we have become: urban, civilized, intelligent and invasive apes.

The work is only beginning. We must accept that we do not know everything, that change may be gradual, that we need to make use of the collective intelligence of stakeholders, to work together – and to fight against our tendency to blame others.

If we consider the installations that each culture has managed to create over the years, and their amazing power, we have proof that it is possible to get people to adopt new behaviour on a large scale. As I have shown above, it is not that complicated to create change and channel behaviour. And it can be done rather fast. A better, different world is indeed within reach, and not so difficult to build, piece by piece, installation by installation.

If we all do our part, we can change the world. Anyone can become a changemaker, individually or in a group. All that is needed is knowledge, method, purpose and work.

You have reached the end of this book. You now have the knowledge and the method. You can start redesigning installations. There is a lot to do. Which activity to improve will you start with? My advice: choose something simple, at home or at work, and do it with someone you like. It is more fun to collaborate.

A social movement starts with two people.

Glossary

action: Consciously controlled motor or mental movement.

activity grid: Describes the activity trajectory step by step, listing the actors, their motives, the components that channel the activity, and the analyst's comments.

activity: What subjects do and how they make sense of it, from their own perspective.

affordance (of an object for a subject): This object's potential for action (for this subject).

behaviour: What subjects do, as described by an external observer.

category: Definition of a set, in comprehension (by the properties of its elements).

community: A group of people with common interests who recognize each other as members of the same community, are aware of their common destiny and have developed some institutions and organizations.

embodied competency: The ability by which the perception of a given object or situation triggers a relevant action. Embodiment implements this process of perception-to-action in the body.

goal: A representation of a desired end state. The subject tries to achieve her goals under the given conditions (the situation).

habit: Behaviour that is repeated so often that it has become routine and is almost automatic in certain situations.

heuristics: Simple procedures for making satisficing decisions or problem solving using only a selection of the potentially available information.

installation: Specific, local, societal settings where humans are expected to behave in a predictable way. Installations consist of a set of components that simultaneously support and control behaviour. The components are distributed over the material environment (affordances), the subject (embodied competencies) and the social space (institutions, enacted and enforced by other subjects). These components assemble at the time and place the activity is performed and channel it.

institution: A set of behaviours expected in a group of individuals in a given context, and the means to enforce them.

know-how: The ability to perform an action to achieve a goal. Comes from having knowledge about affordances and what to do with them to achieve the goal.

knowledge: Ability to describe and recognize categories of objects.

motive: The urge to achieve an inner state which makes one feel balanced or satisfied.

now-what?: The fundamental pragmatic question that an actor is continuously facing as the situation evolves along the activity path. This question becomes especially salient at the natural joints of activity, when one subgoal is reached and orientation to the next step is needed, or when something interrupts the current course of action.

object: To the observer, what appears to act or being acted upon as a unitary whole.

operation: Automatic, routinized movement that takes place beyond the threshold of consciousness (as opposed to action, which is conscious).

organization (human): Socio-technical system binding people in subsets, in an explicit structure with division of labour to achieve a purpose. The subsets are bound by social contracts.

orientation: Considering the situation and choosing a course of action.

point of action: Where and when the behaviour occurs.

procedure: A sequence of steps based on a set of rules.

regulation (s): Content and means of (social) control.

resilience: An installation is resilient if it is able to produce satisficing behavioural activity sequences even if some components are faulty or missing.

role (of a person): The set of behaviours that others can legitimately expect from a person.

satisfaction: the difference between expectations (what you want) and experience (what you get).

satisficing: satisfying minimal expectations.

simulation: 're-enactment of perceptual, motor, and introspective states acquired during experience with the world, body, and mind'.[1]

social contract: The combination of a role and a status ('you do this, you get that').

society: A set of people who consent to the same set of social contracts, and the installations they use. Society comprises the many components of its installations, the social contracts that bind its members, and the values that underlie these contracts.

status (of a person): The set of behaviours a person can legitimately expect from others.

subsidiarity: A principle of regulation whereby issues are dealt with at the most immediate (or local) level consistent with their resolution. Decisions and actions are taken at the local level, unless issues cannot be dealt with at the local level, in which case they are dealt with at the higher level.

system: a set of interrelated entities whose interrelationships enable the system to be maintained as it is, with some resilience.

trajectory of activity: The path from the current state to the final state, by achieving one subgoal at a time. It appears as a sequence of tasks to be solved; each task being addressed by an action.

window of opportunity: A situation where the status quo unfreezes, opening people and organizations to change.

Notes

Introduction

1 Alas, we have been warned long ago, but the problem still badly needs solving; hence this book. See Diamond, J. (2005). *Collapse. How Societies Choose to Fail or Succeed.* Penguin Books; see also Meadows, D. H., Meadows, D. L., Randers, J. and Behrens, W. I. W. (1972). *The Limits to Growth.* Universe Books.

2 Lahlou, S. (2017). *Installation Theory: The Societal Construction and Regulation of Behaviour.* Cambridge University Press.

1 Applying behavioural change

1 Thaler, R. H. and Sunstein, C. R. (2008). *Nudge: Improving Decisions about Health, Wealth, and Happiness.* Yale University Press.

2 Szaszi, B., Higney, A., Charlton, A., Gelman, A., Ziano, I., Aczel, B., Goldstein, D. G., Yeager, D. S. and Tipton, E. (2022). No reason to expect large and consistent effects of nudge interventions. In *Proceedings of the National Academy of Sciences of the United States of America (PNAS)*, 119(31): e2200732119; see also Hallsworth, M. (2023). A manifesto for applying behavioural science. *Nature Human Behaviour*, 7(3): 310–22.

3 Yamin, P., Fei, M., Lahlou, S. and Levy, S. (2019). Using social

norms to change behavior and increase sustainability in the real world: A systematic review of the literature. *Sustainability*, 11(20): e5847.

4 Hertwig, R. and Grüne-Yanoff, T. (2017). Nudging and boosting: Steering or empowering good decisions. *Perspectives on Psychological Science*, 12(6): 973–86.

5 Chater, N. and Loewenstein, G. (2023). The i-frame and the s-frame: How focusing on individual-level solutions has led behavioral public policy astray. *Behavioral and Brain Sciences*, 46: e147.

2 Behaviour is more or less predictable, and the reason why

1 Aumann, R. J. (2006). War and peace. *Proceedings of the National Academy of Sciences of the United States (PNAS)*, 103(46): 17075–8.

2 Gibson, J. J. (1982). Notes on affordances. In E. Reed and R. Jones (eds.), *Reasons for Realism. Selected Essays of James J. Gibson* (pp. 401–18). Lawrence Erlbaum Associates.

3 Adminaité-Fodor, D., Carson, J. and Jost, G. (2021). *Ranking EU Progress on Road Safety. 15th Road Safety Performance Index Report*. European Transport Safety Council.

3 From behaviour to activity

1 Mironenko, I. A. (2013). Concerning interpretations of activity theory. *Integrative Psychological and Behavioral Science*, 47(3): 376–93; see also Nosulenko, V. N. and Samoylenko, E. S. (2009). Psychological methods for the study of augmented environments. In S. Lahlou (ed.), *Designing User Friendly Augmented Work Environments. From Meeting Rooms to Digital Collaborative Spaces* (pp. 213–36). Springer.

2 Boltanski, L. and Thévenot, L. (2006). *On Justification: Economies of Worth*. Princeton University Press.

3 Stanovich, K. E. and West, R. F. (2000). Individual differences in reasoning: implications for the rationality debate? *Behavioral and Brain Sciences*, 23(5): 645–65; discussion 665–726.

4 Newell, A. and Simon, H. A. (1972). *Human Problem Solving.* Prentice-Hall.

5 Haller, R., Rummel, C., Henneberg, S., Pollmer, U. and Köster, E. P. (1999). The influence of early experience with vanillin on food preference later in life. *Chemical Senses,* 24(4): 465–7.

6 Libet, B., Gleason, C. A., Wright, E. W. and Pearl, D. K. (1983). Time of conscious intention to act in relation to onset of cerebral activity (readiness potential). *Brain,* 106(3): 623–42; see also Haggard, P. (2008). Human volition: Towards a neuroscience of will. *Nature Reviews Neuroscience,* 9(12): 934–46.

4 The ethics of behaviour and the golden cage of society

1 Berger, P. L. and Luckmann, T. (1966). *The Social Construction of Reality; A Treatise in the Sociology of Knowledge.* Anchor Books.

2 McNeil, M. C., Polloway, E. A. and Smith, J. D. (1984). Feral and Isolated children: Historical review and analysis. In *Education and Training of the Mentally Retarded,* 19(1): 70–9.

3 Suchman, L. A. (2007). *Human–Machine Reconfigurations: Plans and Situated Actions.* Cambridge University Press.

4 Ostrom, E. (2010). Beyond markets and states: Polycentric governance of complex economic systems. *American Economic Review,* 100(3): 641–72.

5 Schein, E. H. (2013). *Humble Inquiry. The Gentle Art of Asking Instead of Telling.* Berrett-Koehler.

5 What makes people behave as they do: installations and their three layers

1 Lahlou, S. (2017). *Installation Theory.* op. cit.

2 Hutchins, E. L. (1995). *Cognition in the Wild.* MIT Press.

3 Gigerenzer, G. and Gaissmaier, W. (2011). Heuristic decision making. *Annual Review of Psychology,* 62: 451–82.

6 The physical layer: affordances of objects at the point of action

1 Warren, W. H. J. (1984). Perceiving affordances: Visual guidance of stair climbing. *Journal of Experimental Psychology. Human Perception and Performance*, 10(5): 683–703.

2 Marshall, A. (1890). *Principles of Economics* (vol. 1). London: Macmillan.

7 The embodied layer: competences of the subject

1 Uexküll, J. von (1992). A stroll through the worlds of animals and men. A picture book of invisible worlds (1st German edn 1934). *Semiotica*, 89(4): 319–91.

2 See also Bachimont's theory of the medium: Bachimont, B. (2004). *Arts et sciences du numérique: Ingénierie des connaissances et critique de la raison computationnelle*. Habilitation thesis. Université de Technologie de Compiègne.

3 Miller, G. A. (1956). The magical number seven, plus or minus two: Some limits on our capacity for processing information. *Psychological Review*, 63(2): 81–97.

4 Kahneman, D. (2011). *Thinking Fast and Slow*. Farrar, Straus and Giroux.

5 Thorndike, E. L. (1911). *Animal Intelligence; Experimental Studies*. Macmillan.

6 Becker, H. S. (1966). *Outsiders: Studies in The Sociology of Deviance*. The Free Press.

7 Bandura, A. (1977). *Social Learning Theory*. Prentice Hall.

8 Cattaneo, L. and Rizzolatti, G. (2009). The mirror neuron system. *Archives of Neurology*, 66(5): 557–60.

9 Lahlou, S. (2021). Social representations and individual representations: What is the difference? And why are individual representations similar? *RUDN Journal of Psychology and Pedagogics*, 18(2): 315–31.

10 Anderson, K. G. (2006). How well does paternity confidence

match actual paternity? Evidence from worldwide nonpaternity rates. *Current Anthropology*, 47(3): 513–20.

11   Cialdini, R. B. (2009). *Influence. Science and Practice* (5th edn). Pearson Education.

12   Coase, R. H. (1937). The nature of the firm. *Economica*, 4(16), November: 386–405.

8   The social layer: regulation by others and society

1   Lewin, K. Z. (1959). Group decision and social change (1st edn 1947). In T. M. Newcomb and E. L. Hartley (eds.), *Readings in Social Psychology* (pp. 197–211). Henry Holt.

2   Asch, S. E. (1951). Effects of group pressure upon the modification and distortion of judgments. In H. Guetzkow (ed.), *Groups, Leadership and Men* (pp. 177–90). Carnegie Press; see also Sherif, M. (1935). A study of some social factors in perception. *Archives of Psychology*, 27(187).

3   Goffman, E. (1971). *Relations in Public: Microstudies of the Public Order*. Basic Books.

4   Stoetzel, J. (1963). *La psychologie sociale*. Flammarion.

5   Haney, C., Banks, C. and Zimbardo, P. (1973). Interpersonal dynamics in a simulated prison. *International Journal of Criminology and Penology*, 1: 69–97.

6   Lahlou, S. (2008). Identity, social status, privacy and face-keeping in digital society. *Social Science Information*, 47(3): 299–330.

7   Choi, S.-C., Kim, U. and Kim, D.-I. D. (1997). Multifaceted analyses of chemyon ('social face'): An indigenous Korean perspective. In K. Leung, U. Kim, S. Yamaguchi and Y. Kashima (eds.), *Progress in Asian Social Psychology* (vol. 1) (pp. 3–22). John Wiley & Sons.

8   Milgram, S. (1974). *Obedience to Authority: An Experimental View*. Tavistock Publications; see also, for experiments that show the social contract aspect: Meeus, W. H. and Raaijmakers, Q. A. W. (1995). Obedience in modern society: The Utrecht studies. *Journal of Social Issues*, 51(3).

9 The combination of layers: redundancy, resilience and evolution

1 Giddens, A. (1984). *The Constitution of Society: Outline of the Theory of Structuration*. University of California Press.

10 The behaviour change intervention process step by step

1 Duflo, E. (2020). Field experiments and the practice of policy. *American Economic Review*, 110(7): 1952–73.

2 Lahlou, S., Heitmayer, M., Pea, R., Russell, M. G., Schimmelpfennig, R., Yamin, P., Dawes, A. P., Babcock, B., Kamiya, K., Krejci, K., Suzuki, T. and Yamada, R. (2022). Multilayered installation design: A framework for analysis and design of complex social events, illustrated by an analysis of virtual conferencing. *Social Sciences & Humanities Open*, 6(1): 100310.

3 Lahlou, S. (2011). How can we capture the subject's perspective? An evidence-based approach for the social scientist. *Social Science Information*, 50(3–4): 607–55.

4 Jégou, F. (2009). Co-design approaches for early phases of augmented environments. In S. Lahlou (ed.), *Designing User Friendly Augmented Work Environments. From Meeting Rooms to Digital Collaborative Spaces* (pp. 159–90). Springer.

11 Fixing business models and socio-economic platforms

1 Coyle-Shapiro, J. (2002). A psychological contract perspective on organizational citizenship behavior. *Journal of Organizational Behavior*, 23(8): 927–46.

12 Choosing issues, moments, and stakeholders

1 Ariza, A. and Chiappe, G. (2012). Sin celos sí hay amor. Una experiencia latinoamericana para desactivar la violencia intrafamiliar. In *Antípodas de la violencia: Desafíos de cultura ciudadana para la crisis de (in)seguridad en América Latina* (pp. 165–202). Banco Interamericano de Desarrollo – Corpovisionarios.

2 Yamin, P., Artavia-Mora, L., Martunaite, B. and Lahiri, S. (2023).

Installations for civic culture: Behavioral policy interventions to promote social sustainability. *Sustainability*, 15(4): e3825.

14 Tips for the changemaker

1 Hirschman, A. O. (1970). *Exit, Voice, and Loyalty. Responses to Decline in Firms, Organizations, and States.* Harvard University Press.

2 Verplanken, B. and Wood, W. (2006). Interventions to break and create consumer habits. *Journal of Public Policy & Marketing*, 25(1): 90–103.

3 Franks, B., Lahlou, S., Bottin, J. H., Guelinckx, I. and Boesen-Mariani, S. (2017). Increasing water intake in pre-school children with unhealthy drinking habits: A year-long controlled longitudinal field experiment assessing the impact of information, water affordance, and social regulation. *Appetite*, 116: 205–14.

4 Caballero, M. C. (2004). Academic turns city into social experiment. *Harvard University Gazette*, 11 March 2004; see also Tognato, C. (ed.) (2017). *Cultural Agents Reloaded: The Legacy of Antanas Mockus*. Cambridge, MA: Harvard University Press; see also Yamin Slotkus, P. (2020). Leveraging large-scale behavioural change interventions using social norms, civic culture, and installations. Doctoral Thesis. *London School of Economics and Political Science*, 177(4511): 689.

Conclusion

1 Foucault, M. (1978). *Discipline and Punish: The Birth of the Prison.* Pantheon Books.

2 Caballero, M. C. (2004). *Academic Turns City into Social Experiment.* op. cit.

Glossary

1 Barsalou, L. W. (1999). Perceptual symbol systems. *Behavioral and Brain Sciences*, 22(4): 577–609; discussion 610–60.

Acknowledgements

Things that happen in life are not purely accidental; they are a combination of will and circumstance. Take this book. One day in the summer of 2022, John Thompson was having lunch with his friend Olivier Bouin in the courtyard of the Paris Institute for Advanced Study. Seeing me passing by, Olivier invited me to join them and we chatted over coffee. I talked about my work. John said he would be interested in publishing the gist of it in a short book, and he even came up with a title. The very title you see on the cover of this book.

This may seem like an accident, but it is not; it is another of those things that happen by societal design, like almost everything that happens in our lives. One of John's many roles in society is to select authors and publish books, one of Olivier's roles is to bring people together to change the world, and one of my roles is to do research and share my findings. So, we all had latent motives. Then the setting: the Institute for Advanced Study is *designed* to create such productive encounters, and its lunches are famous for such 'accidents'.

Now, if you think of the *whole* chain of events that produced the material book you now hold in your hands, and the preconditions for it, the chain is dizzying. The work behind the book is the result of decades of collaboration by literally thousands of people, places, devices and processes designed with a purpose, of which the above lunch meeting is just one step. Not to mention that other chain that allows you, right now, to be able to read and understand those little black letters on the paper as meaningful.

In fact, this book is about how such chains of events are constructed and how you can change them for the better. Society works because we all play our part, and because the circumstances are set up to *channel* our behaviour to happen as expected.

I cannot do justice in this tribute to the whole social system, of which I am only one cog, and to all those who have contributed to this book at different stages and in many ways, with ideas, criticism, empirical material, emotional, financial or technical support, and all the rest of it. The people who published the book, my anonymous reviewers, I never met in person, but they were important. The same goes for some authors (living or dead) whose contribution was essential. This is the power of societies: that we can still contribute after our death. Thank you all, for this is the product of your collective work!

Then, when I then tried to see without whom this work would not have been possible, I was amazed at the list, just like when you watch the endless credits at the end of a movie. This tells us something about how societies manage to bring together distributed labour, even in the small object that is a book.

So, a big thank you to: Aaron Cicourel, Adelaide Dawes, Alain Berthoz, Albert Bandura, Alena Ledeneva, Alex Gillespie, Alexandre Lahlou, Aleksei Leontiev, Alfred Schütz, Aliénor Lahlou, Andrea Gobbo, Angelo Torre, Anne Garreta, Anne Sullivan, Anonymous Reviewers, Antanas Mockus, Anthony Giddens, Antoine Cordelois, Arnold Tukker, Atrina Oraee, Authors cited in my Installation Theory monograph, Axel Ducourneau, Barbara Cassin, Barbara Rogoff, Barry Rogers, Baruch Spinoza, Beatrice de Gelder, Ben Babcock, Ben Voyer, Benjamin Lee Whorf, Benjamin Libet, Benoît LeBlanc, Bernard Stiegler, Bertrand Pouvesle, Bettina Laville, Björn Wittrock, Bonnie Heptonstall, Bradley Franks, Brigido Vizeu-Carmargo, Bruno Bachimont, Michel Callon, Camilla Serck-Hanssen, Catherine

Bassani, Catherine Grandcoing, Cécile Durand, Champa Heidbrink, Charles Darwin, Charles Lenay, Charles Stafford, Charlotte Andreasen, Christian Baudelot, Christina Garsten, Christopher Boulharès, Christopher Sorensen, Claire Jeandel, Claire-Anaïs Boulanger, Clara Ross, Claude Fischler, Claudine Provencher, Daniel Andler, Daniel Kaplan, Daniel Linehan, Daniel Nairaud, Daniel Povinelli, David Repetto, Denise Jodelet, Dominique Schnapper, Don Norman, Ed Hutchins, Edgar Schein, Edward Thorndike, Elena Samoylenko, Elinor Ochs, Emile Durkheim, Emma Longstaff, Emma Nash, Emmanuelle Honoré, Erving Goffman, Esther Duflo, Etienne de la Boétie, Etienne Wenger, Evie Deavall, Felipe Brescancini, Filippo Muzi-Falconi, François Aveline, François Boulot, François Jegou, Frédéric Basso, Frédéric Worms, George Fieldman, George Gaskell, Gerd Gigerenzer, Gilbert Simondon, Gregory Bateson, Gretty Mirdal, Gustaf Arrhenius, Helena Heaton, Helga Nowotny, Herbert Simon, Irina Nosulenko, Isabel Urdapilleta, Itzhak Fried, Jack Goody, Jacob von Uexkül, James Gibson, James Hollan, James Liu, Jan Aandal, Jean Decety, Jean Lavé, Jean-Claude Abric, Jean-Eric Aubert, Jean-Gabriel Ganascia, Jean-Luc Lory, Jeanne Bottin, Jeongwon Park, Jerome Bruner, Johannes Rieken, John Krumm, John Roberts, John Thompson, Jorge Correia Jesuino, Judy Wajcman, Julia Black, Kate Raworth, Kurt Goldstein, Kurt Lewin, Latif Lahlou, Laurent Thévenot, Lena Samoylenko, Leor Zmigrod, Lev Vygotsky, Liam Delaney, Liliane Ely, Liora Moskovitz, Lisette Winkler, Lucy Suchman, Ludovic Lebart, Ludwig Wittgenstein, Madeleine Akrich, Madeline Sharaga, Marc Mézard, Marianne Hald Clemmensen, Marie-Christine Lemardeley, Marilene Lieber, Marina Everri, Marion Magnan, Mark Lilla, Markus Reinhard, Martha Russell, Martin Bauer, Max Reinert, Max Weber, Maxi Heitmayer, Michel Foucault, Michel Gondran, Michelle Rathman, Mohammad Sartawi, Mohammed Merdji, Monica Zhang, Mylène Trouvé, Nadège Bourgeois, Nicolas Bricas, Nicole Darmon, Nikos Kalampalikis, Nina Jablonski, Olivier Bouin, Olivier Fillet, Pascal Maubert, Pascal Moliner, Pascale Hébel, Patrick Boucheron, Patrick Caron, Patrick Chandon, Patrick Haggard, Patrick Mac Leod, Paul Bach y Rita, Paul

Dolan, Paul Fournel, Paulius Yamin, Pedro Humberto Campos, Peter Blau, Peter Dieckmann, Peter Hanappe, Philippe Fauquet-Alekhine, Pierre-Antoine Badoz, Raouf Boucekkine, Raymond Boulharès, René Amalberti, Richard Lewontin, Robert Aumann, Robert Cialdini, Robin Schimmelpfennig, Roger Barker, Roy Pea, Sabine Boesen-Mariani, Salvatore Aglioti, Samuel Guibal, Sandra Jovchelovitch, Sandrine Morvan, Sarah Kenderdine, Sarah Worthington, Serge Moscovici, Serge Tisseron, Sergei Rubinstein, Sheldon Garon, Shimon Ullman, Shirley Peirce, Sigmund Freud, Simon Goldhill, Simon Luck, Solène de Bonis, Sophie Le Bellu, Stanley Milgram, Stefan Thurner, Steve Bennett, Susan Beer, Susan Michie, Talcott Parsons, Tereza Vrabcova, Terry Winograd, Thierry Coulhon, Tom Reader, Toshio Fukuda, Ubert Bost, Uichol Kim, Ulrike Felt, Valérie Beaudouin, Valery Nosulenko, Victoria Lee, Vivian Loftness, Vlad Glăveanu, Vladimir Barabanschikov, Volker Hartkopf, Will Stubbs, Winston Maxwell, Xavier Baron, Xiaobo Zhang, Yuri Alexandrov, Yves Bamberger, Yves Winkin, Zoe Jonassen.

Apologies to those contributors who are not listed here, be assured that between the moment I wrote this and right now, I must have shaken my head in despair, thinking: how could I forget writing their name?

Finally, I wish to thank institutions for their support: the London School of Economics and Political Science, the Paris Institute for Advanced Study, the European Commission EURIAS Senior Fellowship Programme, with the support of the French State, managed by the Agence Nationale de la Recherche, programme 'Investissements d'Avenir' (ANR-11-LABX-0027-01 Labex RFIEA+).

Index

Page references in *italic* refer to a table/figure